Virtual COLLEGE

A Quick Guide to How You Can Get the Degree You Want with Computer, TV, Video, Audio, and Other Distance-Learning Tools

PAM DIXON

Peterson's

Princeton, New Je

D1367754

Visit Peterson's Education & Career Center at
http://www.petersons.com

Library of Congress Cataloging-in-Publication Data

Dixon, Pam.
    Virtual college : a quick guide to how you can get the degree you
want with computer, TV, video, audio, and other distance learning
tools/Pam Dixon.
        p.   cm.
    Includes bibliographical references and index.
    ISBN 1-56079-629-4
    1. Distance education—United States.   2. University extension—
United States.   3. Correspondence schools and courses—United States.
4. Educational technology—United States.   I. Title.
    LC5805.D59   1996
    378.1'554—dc20   96-41971
                                                                              CIP

Editorial direction by Carol Hupping   Composition by Gary Rozmierski
Production supervision by Bernadette Boylan   Creative direction by Linda Huber
Copyediting by Kitty Colton   Interior design by Cynthia Boone
Proofreading by Joanne Schauffele

Printed in the United States of America

10 9 8 7 6 5 4 3 2 1

To Foster C. Hess,

a life-time learner.

CONTENTS

ACKNOWLEDGMENTS

It is a rare and pleasant occasion when a writer gets the opportunity to break new ground. This book was such an opportunity for me. Of course, "new ground" also means an intensive research trail. I am deeply indebted to the many program directors, teachers, students, and experts with whom I spoke in the course of researching this book. They provided me with contacts, interviews, statistics, and the benefit of their long experience in this exciting field. They made my job not only easy but enjoyable.

Among them, Sally Johnstone at WICHE, Mike Lambert at the DETC, Cheryl Liebowitz at the U.S. Department of Education, numerous people at ACE, Jaci Ward, Pamela MacBrayne, Elaine Sunde, Charlotte Farr, Chris Dede, Leslie Purdy, Braden Kuhlman, John Burgeson, Robert Threlkeld, Dick Vigilante, Glen Wilde, Gearold Johnson, Terri Hedegaard, and William Phillipp Jr. were critically important to this book. Heartfelt thanks to each for patiently fielding my repeated calls and questions.

Also, special thanks to Carol Hupping; her clear vision of this project kept me on target, and she is a writer's dream editor. Margot Maley of Waterside Productions was, as always, a source of encouragement and good advice. Thanks to Joyce Lain Kennedy for her sharp eye and to Amanda Taylor for her elegant manuscript suggestions. Most of all, thanks to Dave for his continual support.

Virtual

COLLEGE

1

BRINGING THE CAMPUS TO YOU

College: It used to be synonymous with campus. But not anymore. Now, you don't have to go to a campus to take classes, get a degree, or obtain a certificate. Now, the campus can come to you. In virtual college you access the courses *when* you want as well as *where* you want. Are you interested?

Melinda Poindexter was. Melinda lives in Port Alsworth, Alaska, a remote village with two airstrips, a school, and seventy-five residents. Through virtual college, Melinda earned her teaching credential despite the isolation, the permafrost, and the 1,000 miles separating her from the nearest university.

Ben Mazza, a Madison Avenue advertising executive living in the heart of New York City, also opted to attend virtual college. Ben earned a professional certificate in a computer-related field. Now his technical savvy gives him a valuable edge over his competition, and he never had to face the wilds of the city or quit his job to get it.

What kind of situation are you in? Do you want to finish college, but you don't have the time? Are you interested in changing careers, but you can't quit your job to go back to school? Perhaps you've been busy raising a family, and you want to brush up on your skills before you enter the workplace. Or maybe you're looking over your shoulder, worrying if you'll be the next one to get laid off.

Whatever situation you're in, if you want to change careers, sharpen your competitive edge, finish high school, make more money, earn a college degree, or get a Ph.D., virtual college can help you

3

accomplish your goals. You can reengineer yourself for the career you really want or the one you really want to keep and advance in. You can go to school and keep your life, too, because convenience and flexibility are the hallmarks of virtual college.

There are millions of students just like Melinda and Ben. *Five million* people a year get their education through virtual college. Did you know that you can attend college dozens of ways, without ever sitting in a campus classroom? It's true. Today "name" colleges and universities offer two-year, four-year, master's, certificate, and even Ph.D. programs—all from a distance. If you want, you can earn that degree, take courses, and improve your life, because your education options are growing faster than you can say "virtual college."

- How much does it cost?

- How long will it take?

- Can I get financial aid?

- Will my employer pay?

- Will I learn as much as I would in a "regular" classroom?

- Do I need to be a technical wizard?

- Will my training or degree mean as much as a degree earned on campus?

- Will I be lonely and without a peer network?

- Am I too old or too young for this?

- How can I tell if I'm looking at a good virtual college program?

- Will I succeed academically?

This book will answer all of these questions. It will give you an insider's look at the terrific distance options you have open to you today, from taking just one course to getting a degree. I'll introduce you to many successful virtual college graduates and students. You'll see what virtual college was like for them and what it will be like for you, both before and after you graduate.

If you're worried that you might not have the discipline, personality, or background for virtual learning, experienced virtual teachers will tell you what real skills it takes to succeed in the virtual classroom. Along the way, you'll hear all the pros and cons of the most popular ways of attending virtual college, and you'll get a peek into the new, sophisticated on-line options now at hand. So read on: find out just how real virtual college is.

WHAT IS A VIRTUAL COLLEGE?

Is it a giant, Oz-like institution, filled with a whirring bank of phones, computers, and video cameras? A huge warehouse filled with anonymous people stuffing assignments into stacks of envelopes? It's neither.

Any educational institution using technology to enable you to break out of the time and space barriers traditionally associated with learning and studying is a virtual college. Technology can be as simple as pen and paper, as in correspondence study, or it can be highly

---

F. Y. I.

WHO CAN BENEFIT FROM VIRTUAL COLLEGE?

You can benefit from virtual college if you:

- want to pursue further education
- want a high school diploma, certificate, associate degree, bachelor's degree, master's degree, or Ph.D.
- work full- or part-time
- live in a remote or a winter-bound area
- have a family at home you care for during the day
- want to upgrade/update your job skills to advance in your career
- want to learn a new career skill while you're still employed in another profession
- need continuing education credits for certificate upkeep and renewal
- want to finish that degree you got so close to finishing but didn't—and then life took over
- are in high school and want to "work ahead" to earn college credit
- are in the military
- travel frequently
- are physically challenged

---

sophisticated, as in courses delivered live over satellite networks. It includes college-level, college-credit courses leading to a degree as well as high school courses, certificate programs, military training programs, corporate training, and seminars.

A number of terms are used to describe virtual college. The most common phrases include distance education, distance learning, home study, and correspondence study. No matter what it's called, though, the distinguishing characteristic of virtual learning and studying is that the education *comes to you*.

Where Are the Virtual Colleges?

It's easy to spot a conventional college; you just look for the building with students milling around. You can't pin down a virtual college

---

F. Y. I.

DISTANCE EDUCATION: THE EXPERT'S DEFINITION

In 1996, the American Council of Education convened a national task force on distance education. The ACE's final report includes its carefully worded definition of distance education as well as a set of guiding principles for distance learning.

"Distance learning is a system and a process that connects learners with distributed learning resources. While distance learning takes a wide variety of forms, all distance learning is characterized by:

- separation of place and/or time between instructor and learner, among learners, and/or between learners and learning resources
- interaction between the learner and the instructor, among learners and/or between learners and learning resources conducted through one or more media; use of electronic media is not necessarily required

The *learner* is an individual or group that seeks a learning experience offered by a provider. The *provider* is the organization that creates and facilitates the learning opportunity. The provider approves and monitors the quality of the learning experience. Providers include schools, colleges and universities, businesses, professional organizations, labor unions, government agencies, libraries, and other public organizations."

From the American Council on Education report "Guiding Principles for Distance Learning in a Learning Society," May 1996.

---

nearly as easily. In contrast to the prototypical on-campus, building-centered classroom environment, a virtual college exists anywhere a home institution (like a college or a business) is delivering educational programs and support to a learner.

Melinda Poindexter's home institution was the University of Alaska. She created her virtual classroom 1,000 miles away in her home via telephone conferencing. Ben Mazza's home institution was New York University's School of Continuing Education. Ben also created his virtual college classroom in his home by using a high-speed ISDN connection to hook up to on-line classes. The virtual classroom can be just about anywhere, from your home to an office to a remote site the school has set up especially for virtual learning. Similarly, an institution delivering the education to you can be anywhere.

Many virtual college programs, like Texas Tech University's high school correspondence study, with 29,000-plus enrollees, are associated with a traditional college. This type of program is simple to understand because in your mind you can attach it to the physical college. Visualizing private, highly nontraditional virtual colleges may be more difficult, however, because these types of schools aren't anchored to a familiar sprawling campus.

Here's an example of what I mean: National Technological University is a fully accredited, highly respected university offering thirteen master's degree programs in engineering. More than 1,400 students currently take courses via satellite at corporate sites like

---

A First Look at Virtual College Offerings

In our first virtual foray, let's peek into the University of Alaska, Southeast, catalog. The U of A is a physical campus, but it also offers a stunning array of distance options.

Here's a sampling:

- an elementary education teacher credentialing program
- an Associate of Arts degree in health information management
- a certificate program in business information systems
- many individual for-credit courses, such as museum studies and business math

You can take the classes through live audio conference, live interactive video, and videotape. If you want to take Aquatic Aerobics, however, you'll have to show up in person!

Hewlett-Packard. Since corporations are providing the classroom space, NTU proper has no need for a large physical building. NTU's physical home is only about 10,000 square feet, and there are about forty employees in the building at a time. The compact, decentralized NTU isn't what most people have in mind when they think "university."

As you explore virtual college programs, you'll discover an enormous variety in types of classrooms and types of delivery. You'll also find virtual college programs in institutions ranging from public universities to private colleges to businesses to the military to churches—and more.

How Many Virtual Colleges Are There?

If you take a look at the distance education offerings listed on the World Wide Web, you'll discover that thousands of private and public virtual colleges exist. If you're not on the Web, you may have read virtual college advertisements in magazines or newspapers. It seems as though every month a new virtual institution is created.

If we define virtual college by the broad ACE definition, we can estimate that at least 3,000 virtual colleges exist. This figure includes all manner of courses, good and bad, available to you via distance education. If we further limit the ACE definition by including only accredited programs or courses, then our estimate drops to about 2,000. (You can learn more about accreditation in chapter 4.) Does this figure sound high to you? In fact, I've been quite conservative. Let's break down the numbers and take a closer look.

- Of the approximately 3,300 accredited colleges and universities in the United States, 1,997 offer courses delivered through the Public Broadcasting System Adult Learning Service. (You can read more about the PBS Adult Learning Service in chapter 2.) That means two-thirds of the higher education institutions in the United States offer at least one form of virtual learning.

- The Distance Education and Training Council boasts a roster of 300 accredited, proprietary distance education schools. There is little to no overlap of these schools with the participants in the PBS program.

- A recent ACE survey has identified approximately 270 distance education programs offered through various colleges and universities. These programs, typically degree programs, differ from the PBS offerings. Again, little overlap occurs.

Best of the West

The Western Governor's University is an ambitious cross-state project slated to launch in 1998 or 1999. Once it's up and running, WGU will offer credentials and degrees via a virtual university that crosses the boundaries of ten western states. The governors are hoping to create a system in which financial aid, course transferability, and tuition are equal for all residents, no matter where the instruction originates. For more information about WGU, contact WICHE. (See On-Line Resources near the end of the book.)

- Private universities accredited through regional or other national accrediting organizations account for an unknown number of schools participating in virtual education. Two examples of virtual colleges known to be in this group include the University of Phoenix On-line and National Technological University.

- There are a number of additional virtual programs offered by private corporations and other business organizations. (I discuss these in more detail in chapter 2.)

What Virtual College Is Not

What you *won't* find in virtual college is often as important as what you *will* find. And given the dramatic changes in distance education since its earliest days, we need to clear away any lingering cobwebs.

Virtual college is not a second-rate learning option. A virtual education is not low quality, lower quality, or second best in any way. Because it is so closely scrutinized, distance ed programs often end up offering higher quality than the same courses in an on-campus setting. You can be proud of any degree or certificate you earn through virtual learning.

Accrediting agencies like the Distance Education and Training Council (DETC) keep standards among distance programs high. Don't take DETC accreditation lightly—the word "rigorous" doesn't do justice to the scrutiny distance education schools endure before receiving accreditation from the DETC. (I discuss accreditation and why it's important in detail in chapter 4.)

Attending virtual college does not mean "vapor" support services. Good virtual colleges don't leave you to struggle through your courses alone. They pride themselves on the extensive student support services that are an integral part of true distance education programs and courses. This means that even if you live hundreds of miles from a college campus or training institution, the institution you're taking your courses from will have carefully planned and prepared for your needs.

Think about some of the following issues. You'll begin to see what I mean when I say virtual colleges must plan carefully for distance students' needs.

- Who will students call when something goes wrong? Will they have an 800 number to use when questions or problems arise?

- How will the students register for courses?

- How will they get their textbooks on time?

- If they have a learning disability, how will their special needs be met?

- What if a student's materials arrive late? How does the student participate in missed classes and make up the work?

Library services are a good example of student services for which colleges must prepare adequately. If students need reference books, articles, or any other library materials, a librarian should be only a toll-free call away. And since students can't very well walk to the campus library, the campus library should go to the student, in one form or another.

In chapter 4, you'll find more information about the hallmarks of a good distance ed program, including what student services should be included as part of your virtual education experience.

Virtual college is not just about technology. Distance ed gives you more options, more flexibility, and more educational opportunity. Virtual college is all about what you're learning and how what you learn improves and changes your life. After an initial adjustment period, the technology you use becomes invisible. Think of virtual college technology as a film projector in a movie theater. When you go to a movie, you focus on the film, not on the equipment delivering the film. It's the same with virtual learning. It's the course that matters, not the technological bells and whistles.

Clearing Up the Correspondence Debate

As I've mentioned, virtual colleges can use any of many technologies to deliver classes to students. One of these technologies includes print, otherwise known as correspondence study. Correspondence study earned a bad name prior to 1950, due to some unethical correspondence schools operating at the time. Despite the dramatic changes in today's correspondence courses, the negative reputation lingers on in some corners. And that's too bad, because correspondence study might just be a very effective learning tool for you.

In yesteryear's correspondence courses, you flew solo, doing independent study via mail, with little faculty-student interaction. You signed up for the course, got a textbook, read it, turned in written assignments, took some tests, and got a grade. Meanwhile, the student-teacher interaction was less than immediate, with feedback on tests and questions taking as long ten to twelve days. If you interacted with other students taking the course, which was rare, that also took days.

Today, the situation has changed. Correspondence courses have added videos and audiocassettes to accompany the printed materials. Instantaneous communication takes place via e-mail discussions with professors, class discussions, and team projects conducted over the Internet or via phone conferences. All of this allows students to interact on a regular basis with classmates and the instructor. Even if a correspondence course doesn't use e-mail, telephones, fax machines, and next-day mail still speed up communication significantly.

Distance Learning: On the Upswing

William H. Philipp Jr., director of PBS Adult Learning Services, estimates that the PBS piece of the distance education pie has been growing at 7 to 10 percent each year. Considering that since 1981 some 3.5 million virtual learners have taken PBS courses, that's no small slice. Other distance education programs mirror this estimated growth rate:

- NTU started in 1984 with a modest 82 enrollments. By the 1995-96 academic year, NTU grew to 5,100 enrollments.

- The Marine Corps Institute grew from 323,844 distance education enrollments in 1984 to 627,365 in 1995.

This kind of growth is good news: Ultimately, you're the one who benefits as more institutions provide virtual college offerings.

F. Y. I.

LOOKING AT THE VIRTUAL LEARNER

If you're expecting to meet a "typical" virtual learner, you may find yourself looking a long, long time. Part of the reason is that there are so many of them. And they hail from all walks of life and educational backgrounds. You'll meet many in this book, and what you'll see is that the most important thing they have in common is that they want to succeed. To give you a quick view of those 5 million distance learners, here are a few facts:

- Student ages range from 13 to 70, with the average age of participants varying dramatically, depending on the individual program.
- Students often work part- or full-time.
- Programs frequently report slightly higher percentages of women than men.
- Convenience is often cited as the number one factor for choosing the virtual option.
- Distance learners are highly motivated to succeed.

WHAT'S IN IT FOR YOU?

What's the bottom line for you?

- The prize of skills and knowledge. The most obvious benefit you gain from grabbing your education from a distance is the education itself. If you do your job and the virtual college does its, you will acquire new knowledge, insight, and skills.

- Convenience. Many students who attend classes at a distance do so because they must. Barriers such as a hectic work schedule, children at home, geography, or weather conditions create the need for a virtual rather than a physical campus setting.

    Convenience can take many forms in distance education. It can mean not having to drive a long distance, or perhaps not having to go out of the house during the winter. It may be the ability to fit a class into the corners of a very hectic schedule. Or the luxury of being able to slow down the pace of a class to meet your learning curve.

Visiting Professors, Virtually

When Dr. Rembert Aranda taught a database management course through New York University's Virtual College program, he brought in the man who wrote the book on the subject—quite literally. Dr. Aranda's database class used a text by Dr. Brian Wilson, arguably the world's top expert in database systems. Because New York University has an on-line setting for its virtual college classes, geographical boundaries disappeared. Dr. Aranda invited Dr. Wilson, who lives in England, to visit the on-line class and exchange ideas with the students. In this case, the virtual college environment allowed the students to benefit from personal access to a top expert whose ideas otherwise would have been available to them only through his book.

- Marketability. You've heard the adage "It's not what you know but who you know." Well, not anymore. Who you know may get you an interview, but landing the job depends on a robust résumé and corresponding work experience.

    Virtual learning helps bolster your résumé's weak spots. It also allows you to "repot" yourself into a better soil and a bigger space so that you can spread your roots out into new areas. Even if you don't have work experience in an area you want to grow into, courses or a certificate can make the difference between a "maybe" and a "yes."

- Pay scale potential. Most employers still reward you for additional education by giving you a raise, a better job title, or both. I'll look more closely at the impact of a virtual education in chapter 5.

- Access to top-rung experts in highly specialized disciplines. You already know today's telecommunications technologies allow teachers and students to engage in a meaningful dialogue despite the distances involved. Taken to the next step, the technology also enables you to connect with hitherto inaccessible experts.

WHAT'S IN IT FOR UNIVERSITIES AND TRAINING ORGANIZATIONS?

Teaching from a distance poses many obstacles for universities. The top-notch programs offer students the same quality of education and student support services (such as library services and counseling) that the on-campus programs offer. But when education is delivered over large distances, say, hundreds of miles away or even overseas, the simplest tasks become mighty complicated, not to mention expensive.

Then why do the universities persist? Because surprisingly, schools gain as much from distance education as students do. Here's a short list of the main benefits universities and others receive from nurturing a virtual program and virtual learners.

- Fulfill a mission. Some remote universities, like the University of Alaska, include in their mission statement the goal of reaching all students, no matter where they may be in that far-flung and diverse state. In such cases, distance education may be the only way for a university to make good on its promise.

- Accommodate population growth. As the world population grows, the earth's total land mass isn't growing along with it. Distance allows students to receive a good education, and it allows the universities to increase enrollment—and income—without spending money on buildings and land.

- Reach a wider student population. Through virtual learning and teaching, educational institutions can gather more potential students who otherwise wouldn't been able to attend classes. This fulfills the schools' altruistic missions, plus it allows them to fill the financial gaps left by students who chose not to go to college immediately after high school.

  Trade programs with other schools to strengthen offerings for students and round out curriculum. Distance technology allows

---

Learning Across State Lines

The University of North Dakota's master of science degree in space studies provides an interdisciplinary view of space studies, including its legal, medical, military, political, and civilian aspects. The program exists only at UND. Because of its uniqueness, the Western Interstate Commission for Higher Education chose to include the space studies program in its Western Brokering Project. This project facilitates resource sharing and cooperation among educational institutions. Students in other states can take UND's space studies degree by videotape, live audio-conferences, e-mail, and live on-line chat.

---

educational institutions to take their best offerings and send entire programs across state borders. This makes it economically feasible to spend money on specialized programs that might not draw enough students from the usual enrollment to make the program worthwhile.

- Attract worthwhile students. Virtual learners greatly enhance the diversity of student populations, bringing with them work experience, maturity, and divergence of opinion valuable to on-campus students and to instructors.

WHAT'S FUELING THE VIRTUAL FIRE?

You have more virtual options today than ever before. Even stodgy universities that have traditionally snubbed distance education are jumping—in droves—on the virtual bandwagon. According to a recent ACE "Campus Trends" survey, 60 percent of public universities said that they plan to offer more courses through distance education programs. For the academic establishment, that's quite a declaration.

Newfangled digital bells and whistles have certainly contributed to virtual colleges' climbing popularity. But so have trends such as an older student population with large educational demands, economic belt-tightening, increased workplace demands, and the globalization of our marketplace. These trends have converged to create a dynamic need for flexible, high-quality, lifelong education.

Technology

The Internet and other advanced telecommunications technologies (such as live desktop videoconferencing over computer networks) are luring formerly reluctant educators into the virtual learning arena. The technology gives educators the flexibility they need in their increasingly hectic schedules. More available educators means more courses and programs for you. More courses means more competition between institutions, and more competition means lower costs. Many of the current exciting advances center on what can be done with computer technology, including the Internet. Finally, technology now allows live, interactive education over long distances at a very low cost.

Computers aren't the only technological force moving distance education forward. Another is live, interactive video delivered via cable or satellite, allowing you to see what's happening, not just read about it on a computer monitor. I'll say more about these and other technologies in chapter 8.

Population Trends

We just don't do things the way we used to, say the experts. We aren't going to college straight out of high school, as we used to. We're taking longer to finish college, and we're often returning to school while working full- or part-time. The older part-time learner is the new majority, and that means educational options need to fit into working people's lives. To do this, colleges are employing an increasing array of virtual college options.

Workplace Needs

It's no secret that today's workplace is tremendously competitive and volatile, and it doesn't look like things will be calming down anytime soon. Most people can't plan on sticking with one career for their entire live. It just isn't feasible in today's workplace. To get the career flexibility you want, you need continual infusions of education over a lifetime, not just once at age 18.

This means people need high-quality education specifically tailored for a life already bursting with responsibility. Since few midcareer professionals are in a position to drop out of a career for a few years of educational relief, the virtual option is very compelling indeed. With virtual college, professionals can get the education they want without leaving the job they need.

Globalization of the Marketplace

The increased demand by business and industry for workers who have a global outlook and, ideally, some kind of global training also fans the fire of distance education. Other than spending time overseas, distance technologies are the optimum medium for making a truly global education possible for time- and geography-bound students.

Now, instead of hopping on a plane, you can hop on-line, hook up to a live videoconference, or use other distance learning techniques to share a class with peers from all over the world. And distance ed won't give you jet lag.

SETTING YOUR VIRTUAL AGENDA

You've had a little peek into the virtual world. As you read this book, you'll learn much more about the possibilities and you'll meet many people like Melinda and Ben. You'll hear specifics about programs that you could take. But before you go any further, take a minute to set your personal goals. Just because virtual options are available and just because "everyone else" is doing it, that doesn't mean it's necessarily right for you.

Know What You Want

Before you hurl yourself into action, ask yourself a few critical questions. Be honest with your answers.

- What do you want to gain from your education?

- What are your career and personal goals?

- How does a virtual education fit into your five-year, even ten-year plan?

It's important to know the answers to goal-oriented questions before you begin any of your educational forays. If you don't have any plans or goals, sit down and figure them out now. Otherwise, you may discover that you've wasted your time and money on something that won't ultimately help you. Only you can decide what you want from your education, but here are some more questions that will help you sharpen your focus. Keep in mind that the best time to decide what you want from your education is before you begin taking classes.

If you're a **high school student**, you're probably reading this book because you're interested in taking college credits early, before you finish high school. If this is the case, key considerations are:

- Can I transfer the credits I earn to the college I want to attend?

- Which courses will benefit me most for the majors I may want to pursue?

- Will these courses satisfy core requirements for all possible majors I am interested in?

- Am I academically ready for a college-level course?

If you are **currently attending a traditional college** and want to mix in distance credits:

- Will my distance credits count toward my degree?

- If I take courses from a different institution, will the credits transfer?

- Am I allowing enough time to complete my distance courses?

If you are a **midcareer professional**:

- What specific skill or special knowledge will I gain from this education? Do the outcomes support my career and life goals?

- Does this course make me more marketable in my profession? If so, how?

- Will this course interfere with my work responsibilities?

- If this course supports my personal and career goals, how do I plan to capitalize on and use the information I gain from it?

If you want to **change careers** and you don't know what you want to do with your life, perhaps you will want to cast your net wide and take many different courses before settling into a degree or certificate program. Conversely, if you're trying to finish a specific degree so you can earn higher pay, then a time aspect enters into your consideration of programs. Otherwise, the questions for midcareer professionals apply to you too.

If you are **pursuing education for self-enrichment** and your aim is to be a twentieth-century Renaissance woman or man, then it's likely that you'll find yourself much less concerned with earning a degree or certificate at the end of your study. You will, however, still need to concern yourself with course quality. Use the guidelines in chapter 3 to determine how well a course stacks up against your ideal.

Look Before You Leap

Be aware that imitation virtual colleges do exist, and you'll want to steer clear of them. The best way to do this is to educate yourself about virtual college. This book will help you with that. In chapter 4 you'll find a complete checklist to help you find the best program for you—and keep you out of harm's way.

How to Use This Book

This book is your guide to what virtual college is really like. It will let you test the virtual waters *before* you get your feet wet. To preview all your options, I suggest that you read the chapters that discuss your areas of greatest concern first; but reading sequentially won't hurt either. And don't sign up for a program before reading chapter 4 from start to finish!

2

WHAT KIND OF VIRTUAL JOURNEY DO YOU WANT TO TAKE?

FIRST THINGS FIRST

Each year I plan a challenging journey that will take me to a wild and beautiful place. Some years that journey takes me to fast, cold rivers. Other years my trek takes me to rare mountain vistas that reveal themselves only after long, difficult hikes.

And each year, before I go anywhere or do anything, I sit at my living room table to mull over the possibilities each journey offers, giving each one a sort of mental test-drive. Ultimately, my decision comes down to my knowing where I want to go and what I want to achieve as a result of going there. Finding out the answers to those and other fundamental questions such as "What's available?" and "How long will it take?" occurs right there at my table, before I ever set foot out of the house or invest the first dime.

Before you start is the right time for you to mull over the questions facing you on your potential journey through the universe of virtual college, and that time is now.

This chapter will help you take a mental test drive. You'll get a good idea of exactly what kinds of trips you can take and how long each will take you to complete. You'll get a broad picture of the types of courses and programs currently available and an overview of the institutions you'll most often find offering them. (For more information about finding specific programs, be sure to read chapter 4.)

While you're exploring what's available, keep in mind that any virtual program will contain many elements to consider. These include how the program is delivered, institutional "clout," and class size. That's why as important as a degree or a certificate is, there's much more to contemplate than just the transcript that you get at the end of the process. (I'll talk about these elements in detail in chapter 4.)

What kind of trip do you want to take? And what do you want to have at the end of it? Do you want to go on your journey to get in better career shape, or do you want to find more knowledge along the way? And how long do you want your journey to take? Do you want to take a 3-hour stroll or a longer, more arduous hike requiring intensive time and effort? These are important questions. Let's find out the answers.

WHO'S OFFERING DISTANCE EDUCATION?

At first glance, it may seem that the only places offering virtual college journeys are academic institutions. But that's far from the truth. Many nonacademic organizations offer distance programs, too. The following information will give you an idea of who's offering courses and where to find the offerings.

Colleges and Universities

While traditional public and private colleges and universities offer the gamut of classroom courses, many also offer some form of distance learning. Colleges and universities offer virtual journeys ranging from a short jaunt (just one course) to a long trek (a Ph.D. program).

Colleges and universities almost always offer virtual college programs through their adult education or continuing education departments. Rarely will you find an entire college or university dedicated to distance offerings.

To find out what distance courses are offered, call the adult or continuing education department. Also, see chapter 4 for reference books and other materials that will help you find program listings.

Trade and Vocational Schools

Trade and vocational schools make for a very tightly focused journey on a straight and narrow path. You may want to travel it if you don't need that university degree for your career or if you don't want to spend the time and money it would take to complete a longer set of courses.

In trade and vocational schools, you get to focus on preparing for a specific profession like culinary arts, hairstyling, or printing. The schools streamline their courses so there's no fluff, and you get into a job quickly, usually within a year.

You can expect to spend anywhere from four weeks to a year in a typical vocational-technical training program. Cost will vary dramatically, depending on the program. An approximate range is from $600 for the shorter programs to $10,000 for longer, more complex programs. To find out how to locate vocational schools offering distance education, see chapter 4.

Business and Industry Seminars and Professional Development Courses

AT&T, IBM, Sun Microsystems, General Motors, and other businesses have caught on to distance education techniques. They've learned that

---

An Example of a College-Level Option

The University of Massachusetts, Dartmouth, offers thirteen full-credit university courses to a worldwide audience through its division of continuing education. The "CyberEd" program uses the Internet and other distance technologies to deliver courses, which include for-credit graduate and undergraduate courses such as personal finance and intermediate English composition. As of this writing, 3-credit graduate courses cost about $400, undergraduate courses about $350, and noncredit courses about $135 for residents and nonresidents.

A Virtual Vocational School

The National Tax Training School offers basic and advanced federal income tax preparation courses as well as courses teaching about capital gains and losses, partnerships, S corporations, and retirement planning. The courses for a certificate in federal income tax preparation take from three months to a year to complete, depending on how fast you work. You'll pay about $275 per course.

---

by linking employees via virtual means for training, they save dramatically on the cost of transporting them across the country.

Up until now, only employees have been able to benefit from virtual in-house training. But a new trend is underfoot. Some businesses are beginning to offer virtual courses to the public that will lead to certificates qualifying them as experts using the products the business manufactures. Many software companies already offer this type of training in-house; only a few offer this training at a distance—so far. Watch for all sectors of distance education to grow dramatically in the next ten years as more businesses catch on.

To find out about such opportunities, talk to your personnel manager and keep up-to-date on journals and magazines within your industry.

Military Schools and Training Institutions

If you're in the military, then you already know that you are required to take all sorts of practical and academic continuing education classes. Military schools, such as the Marine Corps Training Institute and the

---

One Company's Virtual Seminar

Sun Microsystems, a company specializing in computer workstations and other high-tech products, broadcasts four to six live, interactive satellite broadcasts worldwide per year. The courses, called "Sunergy," are free noncredit seminars on the latest computer-related topics. Past seminar topics have included "Next Generation Software for A Wired Planet" and "Creativity in the Digital Domain."

Army Institute for Professional Development, are fully accredited schools that exist to help you meet your continuing education needs. These schools offer practical, no-frills virtual journeys that can help you advance through the ranks, quite literally. You can find out more about them by contacting DANTES, the Defense Activity for Non-Traditional Education Support. DANTES serves as a clearinghouse for much information about training and testing in the military and the Department of Defense. DANTES provides educational testing from high school equivalency to the Graduate Record Exams and more. DANTES can help all military personnel find suitable distance education programs, minimize the loss of transfer credit, and put together a solid external degree plan.

DANTES
Public Affairs Officer
6490 Saufley Field Road
Pensacola, Florida 32509-5243
904-452-1745 or DSN 922-1745

Federal Agencies

Do you work for the government? If so, you may discover opportunities for a few virtual journeys. A very limited number of federal and state agencies offer distance training at this point. Those that do realize how eminently practical it can be.

One government agency using distance learning to its full potential is the Open Learning Fire Service Program, a federal program sponsored by the Federal Emergency Management Agency. By studying via distance education through several different universities, students can earn a bachelor's degree in the fire services field.

Programs like this are very difficult to track down. To find more federal programs, I suggest you read the portions of chapter 4 that discuss on-line searching. I also recommend that you speak with your personnel department for further information.

Religious and Other Nonprofit Organizations

Many religious and other nonprofit organizations operate or own colleges. On a practical level, it is unlikely that you will notice the difference between church- and nonprofit-owned colleges and

Virtual Opportunities for Federal Employees

The Federal Training Network offers live, interactive seminars via satellite. The courses, for federal employees only, are very practical. Past course offerings include "Negotiation Skills," "A Step-by-Step Guide to the Internet," and "Communicating in the Workplace."

nonprofit state colleges. In fact, were you to examine the schools that fall into the church- or nonprofit-owned category, you might be surprised at just how many schools' names you recognize. As with all other colleges, you'll need to be very careful about checking accreditation in this area.

WHAT CAN YOU GET FROM YOUR VIRTUAL JOURNEY?

As I have said before, the biggest benefit you get from virtual college is education. You get to explore a new career path, learn a trade, or update your skills. But along with the education, there's often a "paper" benefit—that is, a degree, a certificate, or additional credits to add to your transcript. You have to decide exactly what benefits you want from your virtual college experience. Only you know if you want or need a paper benefit or just a skill benefit.

Medical School

Loma Linda University is a nonprofit, church-owned institution offering choice distance education options. Its School of Public Health offers a master's degree with majors in health administration, health promotion and education, and international health. To complete the program, non-health professionals need 61 credits; credentialed health-care professionals need 51 credits. Students take classes via a combination of independent study and intensive three- to five-day student-instructor sessions. Most part-time students complete the degree in about three to four years. Tuition is about $325 per credit hour for on- and off-campus students.

F. Y. I.

CONTINUING EDUCATION UNITS

Many noncredit courses are offered for Continuing Education Units, otherwise known as CEUs. Each CEU unit equals 10 hours of instruction. Teachers, nurses, doctors, and many other professionals must accrue a certain number of CEUs each year to keep certificates and licenses valid. Many universities recognize the need for flexible CEUs and offer a good selection of noncredit courses at a distance. If you need CEUs from a distance, check to ensure the credits are approved to apply to your CEU needs before you begin a program.

Look below at the different categories of virtual college end results. Surveying the range of virtual offerings, you'll find individual courses, associate degrees, bachelor's degrees, master's degrees, certificate programs, and Ph.D. programs.

Individual Courses

Individual courses are like a 3-hour walk. You see a path, make a quick decision, and just a little while later, you're done. The reasons for taking a single course are endless. Perhaps you want to brush up on a skill before looking for a new job. Perhaps you want to earn a degree, but you've been out of school a while and you want to take a warm-up course first. Or maybe you couldn't get into all of the courses you needed at your on-site campus, and you want a single course to fill the hole in your transcript.

You can take individual courses on a credit or noncredit basis. Decide prior to signing up what suits your needs best. As always, if you do want to earn college credits for a course, make sure that all credits are transferable. Just as few hiking trails are exactly the same length, virtual courses have varying time requirements. The shortest single course averages a few hours' time for completion (noncredit only); the average course takes a semester.

High School Options

If you're in high school, you can take extra high school courses through virtual college or you can get a head start on college by taking

Exploring Individual Courses

Coast Telecourses produces broadcast-quality individual telecourses and supplies them to colleges and universities worldwide, which in turn offer the courses to you. You can find these Emmy Award-winning courses throughout the United States. You can take the courses for credit toward a degree or for personal enrichment. Each state differs, but in the state of California, the Coast Telecourses fulfill degree requirements and transfer into the California State University system.

"Universe: The Infinite Frontier" is an astronomy course that provides students with an introduction to planets, stars, and all that lies beyond. There are twenty-six broadcast-quality video lessons, with a well-written student guide. The video lessons (which are close-captioned) and student guide mesh closely with a textbook, *Horizons: Exploring the Universe*. This is an example of both a well-designed individual course and a good match between course content and delivery medium.

college-level courses. Believe it or not, at least a quarter million high school students a year partake of both types of virtual high school offerings. Most students are trying to accelerate their graduation date, taking advanced-placement classes, or filling in hard-to-find courses. Other students, particularly those living in small towns, simply want more variety.

The high school options are numerous. Most frequently, you will find high school-level offerings through public and private universities. A few "on-line" high schools currently exist, but they are by and large either highly experimental or for residents of remote areas.

To get high school credits in a distance education situation, you first must obtain permission from your high school. Then select the classes you're interested in taking and apply to the institution offering the classes. After course completion, the class credit will be added to your record through the high school.

If you never finished high school, you can earn your high school diploma this way; see the high schools in the On-Line Resources listings near the back of the book for more information.

College Degrees

College degrees: they're the Holy Grail of most people's educational journeys. At the very least, a college degree punches your basic career

High School Options

The STEP-Star Network offers high school language classes like Japanese I and II and Spanish I and II via live, interactive satellite throughout the United States. STEP-Star also offers 100-level college courses such as Anthropology 101 to high school students. The courses are created through Spokane, Washington's Educational District 101. The high school students don't pay for courses; their local school districts pick up the cost. The network serves about 75,000 students, many of them living in rural areas.

ticket and grants you a certain level of respect. At best, college degrees open doors and bring you bigger paychecks in a profession you want to be working in.

Associate Degrees

Associate degrees are generally two-year degrees averaging around 60 credit hours. (That's if you attend full time.) Your best bet for finding virtual associate degree programs is at one of the 2,000-plus two-year colleges in the United States. You can also find associate degree programs through vocational schools, particularly those dedicated to health, tourism, and computer science.

Expect to spend a minimum of two full years pursuing your virtual associate degree if you have no college experience. If you have college credits, how quickly you earn an associate degree will depend on how much of your previously earned credit transfers in.

Going the Distance for an Associate Degree

Front Range Community College is a fully accredited two-year college in Colorado. Front Range participates in the PBS *Going the Distance* program, which means that students can begin and complete an associate degree program via distance education at Front Range. The college also offers its own virtual programs and courses, such as its AAS virtual degree program in library information systems. According to Steve Tilson, director of distance learning for Front Range, more than 900 students enroll in its distance programs each semester. Costs for these courses are the same as for all other credit courses, which as of this writing is about $50 per credit hour for Colorado residents. For nonresidents, the fee is about $200 per credit hour.

The PBS *Going the Distance* program forms the backbone of many two-year colleges' distance education offerings. To find out if a two-year college near you offers the PBS program leading to an associate degree, check with the extension or adult education office at the college.

Bachelor's Degrees

To earn a bachelor's degree at the end of a virtual journey, you'll need to take a trek of approximately four years of full-time study, or about 125 semester units. Few people complete a bachelor's degree in four years via distance education; however, most students need to work part-time, which adds, on average, another two years to the process. Some students, though, may earn their bachelor's in fewer than four years if they have transfer credits from another institution. You'll find many bachelor's degree programs offered via distance education, particularly technically oriented, business and management, and liberal arts programs.

Master's Degrees

If you already have a bachelor's degree, then you'll be happy to hear that there are many virtual master's programs. Master's programs are short but intensive; they typically take about two to three years of part-time study to complete. This makes earning a master's degree via virtual college a lot like going on a short hike up a very steep hill. The path isn't long, but you'll sure sweat and huff as you travel it.

The most popular areas of study are business administration, engineering, teacher education, nursing, management, and computer science. Depending on the program, you can expect to pay from $3,000

F. Y. I.

THE MORE YOU LEARN, THE MORE YOU EARN

At least that's what statistics gathered by the U.S. Department of Commerce, Bureau of the Census, suggest. In 1995, the median annual earnings of workers age 25 and older rose from around $20,000 for a high school graduate, to more than $30,000 for a person with a bachelor's degree, to $38,000 and up for someone with a master's degree.

Reaching for a B.S. Degree from a Distance

Indiana University is just one of many colleges and universities offering undergraduate degrees via virtual courses. It offers associate and bachelor's degrees in general studies and labor studies through its Division of Extended Studies. Students can pursue the degrees at a distance via independent study, televised courses, and other distance education mediums. Degrees take a minimum of four years to complete, unless you have transfer credit. Then you can finish as in as little as one year, depending on your credits. The average cost is about $80 per credit hour for both in-state and out-of-state students. You'll need 120 credit hours for a bachelor's degree; 60 credit hours for an associate degree.

to well over $10,000 to earn a master's. Be aware that many master's programs require a small amount of time on campus, usually one to three weeks.

Doctorate Degrees

Doctorate programs are the longest haul of all virtual journeys, taking the most time and effort for completion. Virtual doctorate programs lead to a Ph.D. or other advanced degree. Almost all virtual Ph.D. programs have a campus residency requirement of some sort, usually for a minimum of a few weeks. Ph.D. programs require entire summers on campus. Virtual Ph.D. programs take between four and eight years to

Engineering Degrees

The Georgia Institute of Technology offers six master's degrees via virtual college, including health physics/radiological engineering, industrial and systems engineering, and other engineering-and computer science-related fields. Video is the primary means of course delivery, with e-mail and World Wide Web support for instant communication. Most students take an average of four years of part-time study to earn the 45 to 50 credits they need to complete a master's. Classes cost about $270 per credit hour; most classes are worth 3 credits. Your master's degree and transcript from GIT will not indicate that you earned your credits or degree at a distance. It will look just like a traditional student's degree.

Reaching Out for a Ph.D.

The University of Idaho offers a Ph.D. in computer science through its Engineering Outreach program. (It also offers nine master's degrees.) The courses are videotaped during live class sessions and then sent to distance students. U of I has a two-semester residency requirement for the Ph.D. program, though it will review the requirement on a case-by-case basis, so there is some room for flexibility. The graduate program requires 78 semester hours. The cost is about $312 per credit for out-of-state students and from $141 to $153 per credit for in-state students near one of the university's remote instruction centers.

complete, with the trend toward longer rather than shorter completion times. Expect to pay anywhere from $7,000 to more than $20,000 to complete a Ph.D.

Certificates

Even if you already have a degree, it's likely that you can benefit from a certificate. The workplace trend today is toward certification. Everyone from professionals to technical workers suddenly seems to need some proof of basic competency, and a certificate is a simple way to assure others of your respectable baseline of knowledge. Certificates require a range of one week to one year of study; the time varies by program and topic.

Certificates come in many varieties. Some professions, such as teaching, insist on a professional certificate—without it you can't enter the field. Other certificates relate to a very specific area, such as a

Keeping Up-to-Date

California State University, Chico, offers a certificate of professional achievement in emergency medical services administration, designed for people who want to advance in the EMS profession and for administrators who want additional training. Students must complete two EMS courses via audio-conferencing and videotapes and a field practicum in order to complete the certificate, which takes 9 credits at a cost of $250 per credit hour.

particular computer language or a vocational skill. A number of professions that have never had firm standards for job entry are now considering making certification mandatory.

Some fields demand more than one certificate because of the fast pace of change and development. Nursing, for example, requires certificate upkeep due to constant advances in medicine. People working in fields such as computer science go after multiple certification as a way of proving skills and staying competitive.

WHAT CAN'T YOU GET?

Before you run for your checkbook and sign up for a virtual journey of any length, know that despite the wide variety of offerings available to you, virtual college doesn't bring every possible degree or course to you.

Some courses just don't translate well at a distance. Sometimes it's better to get your hands dirty and experience the course in a physical setting. Would you have wanted your dentist to have learned his or her craft entirely by videoconferencing? Many life science courses require hands-on learning, so these courses are not always found in virtual colleges.

You're in luck if you're looking for courses in subjects such as business, writing, nursing, computers, mathematics, philosophy, library sciences, and liberal arts (to name only a few). These types of offerings abound.

3

QUALITY CONTROL: HOW DOES DISTANCE EDUCATION MEASURE UP?

COMPARING DISTANCE EDUCATION WITH ON-CAMPUS EDUCATION

In this chapter, we'll look at some comparative test scores of on-campus and distance students that help indicate the relative quality of distance ed. We'll consider the all-important distance education "image factor": how employers and peers will be likely to view your distance education. And finally, you'll peek into the lives of distance ed graduates to hear how they are faring in the real world with their distance ed degree.

Don't assume anything about the quality of your virtual education; go for all the facts you can find. This chapter is a good starting point.

A Look at Some Statistics

Traditionally, tests are used to determine how well you have learned a concept or a skill. They are a time-honored way of proving knowledge.

But tests have their limitations. Think about it: Does one test (particularly a standardized test) tell the whole story about you? No way.

We're about to look at the results of some tests. We're going to compare test scores between on-campus and distance students in three major areas to see how distance students measure up—literally—to on-campus students. But before we look at our first test score, I want to emphasize that in addition to the differences inherent in learning at a physical distance from campus, student motivation, age, personality factors, and work experience all affect students' test scores.

Graduate-Level Comparisons

Professor William Souder had the perfect opportunity to compare distance ed to traditional education. He taught, in one semester, the same graduate-level course at three different campuses. Two campuses were traditional (Georgia Tech and the University of Alabama); one was virtual (National Technological University, delivered via satellite). Best of all for comparison purposes, this situation eliminated one of the biggest variables: different teachers for on-campus and distance versions of the same course.

Looking at all the students' GMAT and GRE scores prior to the beginning of the course, Souder found no significant differences between the on-campus and distance learners. But he did find other interesting differences. Going in, the NTU students had the highest grade point averages and the most work experience; they were also older, on average, than the on-campus students. (I'll talk about other characteristics of distance students in chapter 7.)

At the end of the course, Souder graded the exams without checking the students' names and home schools so he wouldn't be biased. He discovered that although he had taught precisely the same course during the same time frame to all the students, the scores differed significantly. The NTU students scored highest on the final exam, with a mean grade of 95.1; University of Alabama students scored 93.9; and GA Tech students scored 91.6.

Based on exams, term papers, and homework, Souder concluded that the distance learners performed as well or better than traditional learners in the same program. He also found that the distance learners in particular gained valuable social skills and a peer network, all of which were facilitated by learning at a distance.

Bachelor's- and Master's-Level Comparisons

Each academic year, the University of Phoenix charts a comparison between its on-line and its on-campus students, with an eye toward comparing scores in identical programs. While its statistics were not the result of a tightly controlled, full-on research study, the numbers do indicate what other distance program administrators all over the country told me informally: distance students score as well as or higher than on-campus students in their classes.

The table here shows us some statistics the U of Phoenix has collected. While the numbers indicate positive test score gains for learners at a distance, keep in mind that many variables lie behind the figures. On-line students are older, tend to be more motivated, and have more work experience. All of these factors can contribute to higher grades.

MEAN MAJOR-FIELD ACHIEVEMENT SCORES FOR ON-CAMPUS AND ON-LINE STUDENTS

| | Pretest Score | | Posttest Score | |
| | B.S. | | B.S. | |
Program	Business Admin.	M.B.A.	Business Admin.	M.B.A.
On-Campus	26.5	41.5	37.1	53.9
On-Line	34.73	51.2	43.5	62.4

Source: The University of Phoenix

High School Comparisons

Researchers Dr. Elaine Martin and Dr. Larry Rainey decided to compare a distance and a traditional high school class in human anatomy and physiology—not a cakewalk class, either way. The researchers, who conducted their experiment at seven different high schools, took elaborate care to match variables among students, teachers, and content. The distance class was taught via interactive satellite, with videotapes available for students who missed a class. The traditional class was taught on-campus, like standard high school courses. Both classes used the same curriculum and materials.

The researchers, who originally thought there would be no great difference between the scores, were surprised when they got the results

A Drawback of a Virtual College Pioneer

Leonard Simon graduated from the University of Phoenix Online with an M.B.A. in 1995. After he earned his M.B.A., his employer immediately gave him a $3,000 bonus. That's not a bad start. Leonard says that he was able to use his learning on the job immediately and that his degree has really helped him in his work.One thing Leonard doesn't like about his distance degree, though, is that, as he says, "It's not a Harvard M.B.A.—it doesn't have the same name recognition factor." Also, Leonard says he'll be glad when more people learn about virtual college and the on-line world so he doesn't have to explain how on-line learning works and how effective it can be.

back. As the box shows, the distance and traditional students' pretests were practically identical in score. But the final exams, or posttests, revealed that the students who took the class at a distance earned much higher scores than the students who took it traditionally.

ACHIEVEMENT TESTS MEAN SCORES FOR HIGH SCHOOL STUDENTS

Pretest		Posttest	
Distance Students	24.06	Distance Students	33.39
On–Site Students	24.65	On–Site Students	27.61

Source: *Student Achievement and Attitude in a Satellite Delivered High School Course*, Martin & Rainey

How Distance Education Stacks Up with the Leading Edge

Now we know how a sampling of distance ed measures up to traditional on-site teaching. But how does it compare to the newest ideas in education? Marvelously.

Did you ever moan to your teacher, "But why do I need to know this? I'll never use it in real life!" Your teacher might not have had much sympathy for you back then, but a good number of educators and researchers would today. A move is on to anchor teaching to real-life or at least realistic situations so that what the student learns has some meaning and context.

You may not like learning that math equation any more than you used to, but at least you'll know why you're learning it and how you'll use it in "real life." You'll hear experts use terms such as "constructivism," "situated learning," and "active learning" to describe the latest education trends, in both distance and traditional education. According to the newest theories, a teacher doesn't stamp learning into you by endless drill. Instead, he or she facilitates your learning as a coach and guide. You learn by doing, placing your learning experiences in a real or simulated setting. It's much like learning to fly by using a simulator, not by listening to 20 hours of lectures about flying.

In fact, the new technologies used in distance learning help learners become more involved in the learning process. Here are a few ways in which distance ed measures up to the new way of thinking about learning:

- Since they don't have to quit their jobs to attend classes, distance learners who are working can take courses that directly meet their workplace needs. According to an interview with Lionel Baldwin, the president of National Technological University, 87 percent of NTU students report that what they learn in their courses can be immediately applied to their jobs. This lines up with what distance learners told me in my interviews with them. (NTU is a degree-granting institution that operates entirely at a distance, offering courses via satellite.)

- In face-to-face learning, an average of 80 percent of the verbal exchange consists of the teacher talking to the students. In some distance ed programs that extend the classroom without any changes, this same percentage applies. But in on-line classes, the teacher accounts for only 10 to 15 percent of the verbal exchange; he or she acts as a facilitator of knowledge rather than as knowledge's sole purveyor. In this case, the distance difference allows teachers and students to break out of traditional teaching-learning molds.

PERCEPTIONS: THE VIEW FROM OUTSIDE

You know the adage: You can't judge a book by its cover. How does distance ed stand up to the critical "cover" tests: on the job, in interviews, and in pursuit of further schooling?

On the Job

Distance education's image is very good on the job. In today's world, if you have a degree or a certificate, you have more points in your favor. It's always to your advantage to have a degree, whether you earned it at a distance or traditionally. In some instances, your distance degree may be just the impetus your employer needs to give you that raise or promotion you've been waiting for. Also, don't overlook the fact that you can translate the telecommunications skills you learned as a distance learner to value-added business benefits. For instance, you can introduce a business program in which you use your polished teleconference and videoconference skills to serve remote customers more effectively and at much lower costs.

Earning education credits while working shows that you're keeping your skills and knowledge current. In today's fast-moving world, marketability is as much about how well you keep up-to-date as about what you've done in the past. And everyone knows that it takes discipline and motivation to earn a degree, especially when you're already working full- or part-time. When you pursue a degree while working, you demonstrate those positive qualities to your boss while bringing new knowledge to the job.

Employers by and large look favorably upon degrees earned at a distance. Unless you make a point of it, the main thing employers notice is not how you earned your degree but whether you *have* the degree or the training. A survey conducted by the Distance Education and Training Council reveals some specifics about how employers feel about training and degrees earned at a distance:

- 94 percent of employers surveyed said that distance graduates compared favorably in skills, knowledge, and attitude with graduates of traditional programs.
- 97 percent of employers said they would encourage others to enroll in distance ed programs to increase their job competence.

The Corporate Response

Richard Vigilante, director of the Information Technologies Institute at New York University, says he has never had a problem with corporate employers questioning the value or validity of NYU's on-line certificate program after they've spent a little time investigating it. At about $8,200, the NYU certificate is not inexpensive. Employers offering tuition reimbursement want to know that they aren't throwing their money at something less than the very best. If employers are skeptical about, or just unfamiliar with, distance education, Vigilante shows them the intensive, detailed course syllabus and explains the electronic learning process. That gets employers interested and on the students' sides.

Handling Interview Situations

If you've interviewed for a job, you already know that employers focus much more on asking you about the specific skills and experience you bring to the job than on how you earned your degree or certificate. Think about it: When was the last time you were asked during an interview, "Did you take your courses on-campus?" Unless you state on your résumé that you earned your degree or certificate at a distance, the question will probably never come up.

On the other hand, you may want to mention that you've studied at a distance. In some professions, your technical distance learning skills translate to more on-the-job skills. Keep in mind that the education community isn't alone in learning how to do things at a distance—the business community is pursuing this route as well. In fact, much of the technology (such as videoconferencing) used in education was first used in business.

So consider adding information about how you earned your degree to your résumé, depending on your profession. (Be sure to check out the Top Q's and A's in the back of this book for ideas about how and when to add distance information to your résumé, and for interviewing tips.)

Applying to Grad School with a Distance Undergrad Degree

Here is where your diligence in choosing a high-quality program will really pay off. (See chapter 4 for details on how to choose a good

Good Distance Ed Students = Good Distance Ed Teachers

According to Elaine Sunde, director of the Office of Outreach and director of the University of Alaska, SE Sitka campus, if you graduate from the U of A distance system with an elementary education teaching credential, you'll be snapped up in a second. "School districts really prize our distance graduates," says Sunde. And no wonder: in Alaska, many tasks—educational and otherwise—need to be carried out at a distance. Someone who's earned teaching credentials at a distance is going to be well prepared to teach at a distance.

distance program.) If you have chosen to attend an accredited distance undergraduate program, then you should have no problem applying to graduate school and getting accepted (provided you earned good grades, of course, and your degree matches the prerequisites for the graduate program you're trying to enter).

If you have any doubts about applying to graduate school with the distance undergraduate degree you're planning to get, the best time to assuage your fears is before you sign up for the program. Decide on three or four target graduate schools, then call the admissions office of each and ask if there is any policy, pro or con, regarding degrees earned at a distance. Most graduate schools do not discriminate against them.

When I called various grad schools and asked about this topic, most replied that as long as the program was accredited, there wouldn't be a problem. (For a discussion of accreditation, refer to chapter 4.) If you have your heart set on attending a particular graduate school, you may want to go the extra step of getting the school's assurance in writing.

QUICK QUALITY FACTS

While looking at the studies and speaking with several admissions officers, program coordinators, professors, and education experts, I gathered some facts about how distance ed stacks up:

- On tests, papers, etc., the majority of distance students score as high as or higher than their peers in on-campus classes.

- Learning at a distance allows students to forge new, positive learning patterns in line with today's ideas about education.

- Distance students typically interact more in their distance courses than do students in on-campus courses. The increased participation enhances learning in many subtle ways that don't always show up on tests (for example, higher self-esteem, better social skills, better problem-solving skills).

- In the workplace and when interviewing for jobs, it's not unusual for distance graduates to have to explain what learning at a distance entails. But the effort is worth it; some job hunters report that distance ed helped distinguish them positively from other candidates and peers.

- Employers working with distance graduates rated distance learners positively.

4

FINDING AND CHOOSING YOUR VIRTUAL PATH

ARE YOU READY?

Use this chapter as your virtual college field guide. It'll show you what you need to have before you begin your college selection process and how to uncover information about programs. You'll find the key questions you need to ask as you select a virtual college and a checklist that will help you make sure you don't leave anything behind or get caught unprepared. You'll also find a list of danger signs so you can avoid any trouble lurking in unexpected places.

Do You Have the Equipment You Need?

Getting ready to attend virtual college involves more than purchasing a new notebook and a pen. For some programs, you may only need access to a mailbox and postage. Other programs will require that you have a telephone, a videocassette player, and a computer. To access an audio-conference system, for instance, you'll need a telephone with a good mute button and a speaker phone. For an on-line system, you will need a computer with certain features and software. Let the college or program tell you what you need. (See chapter 8 for a detailed discussion of delivery methods in common use today and the specific skills and equipment you need to be effective with each.)

Do You Have the Academic Skills You Need?

This may surprise you, but over and over studies reveal that the number one factor behind virtual students' success is a commitment to completing the program—not academic skills. If you are absolutely determined to finish your degree, take that course, or earn a new certificate, then it is very likely you will.

If you feel unsure of your academic skills in areas such as writing, researching, and studying, talk to the school. Ask if you can take some brush up courses before you begin your program in earnest. You may also find that the combined effects of time and maturity have created a more determined and studious you.

Do You Have Enough Financing?

It's no secret that a good education is expensive. Look very carefully at your ability to finance not just one part of a virtual program but the whole undertaking. If you know that you can't afford a $20,000 education, find a way to finance it before you get involved, or choose a less expensive program. Don't start something you can't finish. (I'll discuss special considerations and methods for financing your virtual education in chapter 5.)

GET A GOOD GUIDE TO HELP YOU: HOW TO FIND AVAILABLE OFFERINGS

You know information about specific virtual colleges must be available somewhere, but where? If you could only find the definitive list. . . . Unfortunately, there isn't one; so many virtual colleges, programs, and courses are starting up that it is difficult to keep up with them all. Trying to list every offering is like trying to hit a moving target. No one guidebook lists every program, so it's important to use all the different ways of finding a program, not just one.

Harvard Law School from Home?

Seven Harvard Law School professors are developing an independent virtual college program called the Bridge Program in conjunction with Lexis Nexis. According to Todd Rakoff, a Harvard Law School professor working on the project, the program will provide virtual materials for a full first-year law curriculum.

The curriculum is highly interactive and is delivered via videotaped lectures and electronic casebooks. The professors' intention is for other colleges to use the materials in conjunction with (not as a replacement for) their own programs.

The first stage of the Bridge Program, which came on-line in July 1996, includes materials for courses such as "The History of Legal Thought in the 20th Century" and "The Use of Analogical Reasoning." Who knows—when the professors finish their curriculum, maybe Harvard will offer the courses at a distance, too.

Adopt this rule of thumb: No matter how you hear about a program and no matter how great a program looks in a glossy brochure, be sure to thoroughly examine the school and the program before you sign up.

Guidebooks

The classic and perhaps the easiest way of uncovering existing programs is to check a print reference guide that lists programs for you. There are several excellent guides:

- *A Guide to Distance Learning*, Peterson's, Princeton, New Jersey. This reference guide lists accredited programs from correspondence to on-line to satellite delivered. The guide is meticulously researched and extremely useful for finding available degree and certificate programs.

- *Bears' Guide to Earning College Degrees Non-Traditionally*, John Bear and Mariah Bear, C & B Publishing, Benicia, California. To my knowledge, this is the only guide that gives a detailed listing not only of accredited colleges but of "degree mills" to avoid. It also contains an excellent discussion of accreditation.

- *College Degrees by Mail,* John Bear and Mariah Bear, Ten Speed Press, Berkeley, California. This volume lists 100 accredited schools that offer degrees by home study.

On-Line Information

Another good way to uncover virtual college programs is by going on-line. Internet information can be updated quickly and frequently, making it more current than print information. But before you charge on-line, expecting to find everything you need, be aware of two problems.

On-line information won't be neatly gathered into a book for you. You have to forage for the information you want, which is very time consuming. Also, don't be seduced by an enticing Web page. While many excellent and credible schools have their own Web pages, so do some less than reputable schools. Be especially careful about programs you read about on the Web and cannot find information on anywhere else. You'll find a virtual college checklist in this chapter; use it! Don't give any money to a school until you've gone through the checklist.

If You're an On-Line Expert

If you have access to the World Wide Web and you know how to look for information on the Web, then I suggest the following search strategies for you, which will take you beyond On-Line Resources.

- Perform a key word search for the specific names of colleges you're interested in. Look in the continuing education or adult ed sections to find distance programs and read the most current information.

F. Y. I.

ON-LINE RESOURCES

In On-Line Resources near the back of this book, you'll find addresses of numerous Web sites that will provide you with virtual college program information. The listings will save you a lot of hunting and gathering time.

- Perform a key word search for "distance education." You'll receive as many as a couple hundred thousand entries, but if you have the patience, you might find that golden piece of information you are looking for.

- Sign up for the Listserves found in On-Line Resources. Use them to network and ask questions about specific programs you're interested in—*after* you've done your homework and checked print references and looked on-line for information.

If You Don't Have Access to the Web

Try a local public or academic library. (Many offer free or low-cost public access to the Web.) Ask someone to help you open the addresses I've listed in On-Line Resources. From there, you'll be on your way.

Other Information Sources

Many students find virtual college programs through print advertisements in their local paper or in national magazines. Many credible schools advertise in this manner. Don't overlook the obvious: the next time Sunday rolls around, buy your local paper and look in the classified section under the jobs and careers headings.

Also, if you've heard about a program through word of mouth, or if you have a specific university in mind, call up the university's information department and ask to speak to the school of continuing education about the distance programs it might offer.

Professional and trade associations often have lists of member schools. One such association, the Distance Education and Training Council, can send you a list of more thans 300 accredited distance education schools:

Distance Education and Training Council
1601 18th St., NW
Washington, DC 20009
202-234-5100

KEY CONSIDERATIONS IN CHOOSING A VIRTUAL COLLEGE

See the fourteen key points you need to consider as you evaluate virtual colleges. Then read the Student's Virtual College checklist later in this chapter. You'll have a clearer idea of what you want from a virtual college, and you'll know the questions you need to ask before you sign up.

But first, read about accreditation. Accreditation, or the lack thereof, can dramatically impact the usefulness of your virtual education, and there is much misunderstanding about the issue.

Accreditation

Why is accredidation important to you? If you attend a virtual college without proper accreditation, you may not be able to receive certain types of financial aid, and you also may lose out on professional

The Virtual College Principles of Good Practice

The Western Cooperative for Educational Telecommunications created "Principles of Good Practice for Electronically Offered Academic Degree and Certificate Programs" as a baseline for quality virtual programs. The document serves as an important guide for checking the quality of programs you're considering. Here are some excerpts:

- An electronically offered degree or certificate program is coherent and complete.
- The program provides for appropriate real-time or delayed interaction between faculty and students and among students.
- Qualified faculty members provide appropriate oversight of the program electronically offered.
- Enrolled students have reasonable and adequate access to the range of student service appropriate to support their learning.
- Accepted students have the background knowledge and technical skills needed to undertake the program.
- Advertising, recruiting, and admissions materials clearly and accurately represent the program and the services available.

licensing down the road. Attending an unaccredited school doesn't necessarily mean you'll get a poor education. But you do run the risk that the school may be subpar in many areas. You won't know until you attend, because accreditation is a very general form of quality control. Also, in fields like nursing and law, if you attend an unaccredited college, you may not be able to get a license *even if you have a degree.*

I hope I have your attention, because now I want to lead you through a thicket of thorny details.

Accreditation Is . . .

Accreditation is a voluntary, expensive, and excruciating process an institution goes through to show that it meets certain minimum standards of educational quality. Students attending an accredited institution should be able to trust that the curriculum is appropriate, faculty members are well trained and competent, facilities are well oiled and up to par, appropriate student services are in place, and a host of other elements are in proper working order.

Should is the operative word here. Unfortunately, not all accreditation is created equal. Some accreditors are better than others at evaluating virtual colleges. And then there is the entire issue of approved versus nonapproved accreditors.

This last is a very important point: you must have credible accreditors accrediting the college or institution. That's why, before enrolling, you must check to see if the college is accredited and then immediately check to see who is accrediting the college.

Who Can Legitimately Accredit?

Many accrediting bodies exist. Some are valid, some aren't. Currently, there are only two organizations that can approve accreditors: the United States Department of Education and the Commission on Recognition of Postsecondary Accreditation (CORPA). Both of these organizations will supply you with a list of approved accrediting agencies:

United States Department of Education
Bureau of Postsecondary Education
Accreditation and State Liaison Division
Washington, DC 20202
202-708-7417

CORPA
One Dupont Circle, NW, Suite 305
Washington, DC 20036
202-452-1433

Professional Accreditation

Let's say you find a school you want to attend. You check its accreditation. It's accredited. You check its accreditor with the Department of Education and with CORPA, and you find it listed as approved by one or both. Now comes the important question: Is the department you want to attend accredited by a professional association? Sometimes this is a critically important question; sometimes it's not important at all. It depends completely on your degree. Let's look at two professions.

Teaching: Prospective teachers should always see to it that the virtual school they'll be attending is accredited by an approved accreditor. It's a good idea to see if the teacher education department is accredited by the National Council for Accreditation of Teacher Education, the professional association that accredits teacher education colleges, virtual and traditional. Only one third of teacher education departments are accredited by NCATE right now. Although NCATE accreditation does not determine your ability to get a teaching certificate, it will assure you of a very high-quality teacher education program. Also, according to NCATE, some school boards are only hiring teachers who have their degree from an NCATE-approved school.

Law: Everyone who wants to practice law needs to pass the bar exam. In all but four states, in order to even sit the bar exam you will need to have graduated from a law school accredited by the American Bar Association. So, if you are looking at virtual law programs, you must ask first about general accreditation, then about ABA accreditation of the virtual law school. Many medical- and health-related professions have similar professional accreditation requirements.

F. Y. I.

TIPS FOR STUDENTS FROM AN ACCREDITOR

Distance education is turning accreditation upside down. When faced with a virtual campus, many approved accrediting agencies just don't know what to do with all the innovation and technology. Some are more up-to-date than others, with better standards by which to judge virtual colleges. Currently, there aren't any hard-and-fast nationally applied standards for virtual colleges. Because of the lack of equal standards, even approved accreditation can mean different things, depending on how good the accreditor is and how much that accreditor knows about virtual colleges. What's a student to do?

Steve Parker is executive director of the Accrediting Council for Independent Colleges and Schools, an approved accrediting agency that accredits private colleges. Very familiar with virtual college issues, he advises students to ask the accredited institution the following questions:

- What is the percentage of teacher interaction?
- What's the objective of the program?
- What's the success rate of graduates?
- What's the completion rate?
- How many graduates are placed in their fields of training?

Parker also recommends that you ask the institution for a list of students, both current enrollees and graduates of the program, and talk to at least three of them about the quality of their program.

The Fourteen Key Points for Evaluating Schools

1. Faculty Credentials and Training

The quality of the faculty on board can make or break a distance program. What you're looking for are faculty members who have appropriate degrees and experience to teach in the field, who are trained specifically to teach at a distance. Many, but not all, virtual colleges give teachers specific instruction for working with the distance technology and working with students at a distance, so be sure to ask.

2. Student Population

Because virtual programs can cross geographical boundaries, you often have the opportunity to learn among a more diverse student body than if you were to attend on-campus classes. This may or may not be an important factor to you. If it is, ask the school you are considering for a breakdown of student population. The school or institution should be able to give you a good idea of where students live, their average age, and the "feel" of the student body. Expect to find wide variations in age and background.

3. Library and Research Resources

The availability of library and other research resources is a critical area for you to investigate as a virtual student, particularly if you are pursuing a degree program. The more challenging the program, the more resources you will need. Various institutions will provide library and research services in different ways, depending largely on the programs or courses they offer. If an institution can't offer appropriate library or research services to virtual students, it will request that you spend time on campus. You'll see this residency requirement most frequently in Ph.D. programs.

Beware of colleges that overrely on the Web for library research. If you ask a college admissions officer about the school's distance library program and he or she replies, "Oh, we use the Web. Our students can find almost everything they need on it," consider another school. As

---

Learning More "Business Savvy"

Kevin Kimma lives in San Jose, California, in the heart of an area widely known as Silicon Valley. Kevin already has a bachelor's degree, and he has a good job at Octel as a quality systems manager. But to advance paywise, Kevin needs management skills and much more of an ineffable quality he calls "business savvy." When he looked at the half-dozen M.B.A. programs in his geographic area, Kevin realized that if he stayed local, he would be getting the same education as his competition. So after looking around at several distance ed options, Kevin chose to earn his M.B.A. from the University of Phoenix on-line via its computer-delivered program.

According to Kevin, his peers in on-line classes are from all over the United States, and most important for him, from diverse business backgrounds. Kevin has used his on-line peer network to help him creatively solve problems in his current job. Kevin says that taking a step out of a strong local culture is the best thing that he's ever done. Of course, having his M.B.A. won't hurt either.

---

wonderful as the Web is for general research and information finding, it cannot replace the "paper" research you will find at an academic library.

For a degree program, the bare minimum library and research services a distance learning institution should provide are:

- access to the institution's complete library catalog, either on-line or in person

- access to the full range of electronic reference materials, such as databases, that an on-campus student would have

- access to print periodicals, journals, books, case studies, and other physical or audiovisual materials (such as films and cassettes)

- a program of library instruction. Students shouldn't be left without key library search skills and strategies.

- a reasonable turnaround time to get materials to distance students. One month is too long, but students who have procrastinated shouldn't expect materials to arrive within hours, either. One to three days is the average time for requested material to be sent to you. Copyright issues can pose a big snag to getting library resources, particularly journal articles. Some articles and case studies cannot be photocopied unless you pay a fee or royalty, and some resources cannot be photocopied at all. Libraries need extra time to resolve these difficulties, which can delay turnaround time—another reason to plan ahead.

4. Student Services

If you are taking a single course from an institution, it is unlikely that you will receive extensive student services. But if you are in a degree or certificate program, you should have access to such student services as career counseling, tutoring, educational testing and counseling, and technical support. Ask what student services are available to you as a distance student and request a written list. That way, there won't be any surprises.

5. Technologies

You see a program you want. You check out the quality and reputation of the home institution. You apply and are accepted. You're ready to go. Then the first day of classes arrives, and you discover that you can't stand the way the course is arriving at your virtual classroom.

How the course comes to you impacts your experience on every level. A course can work really well or really poorly, depending on how it is delivered. And what may sound good in a catalog may not look or sound as good in practice.

Make sure the method of delivery used is appropriate for the course and is as advertised. If, for example, you're taking a biology class at a distance, you would surely want a visual medium at some point in the course. If you're studying music appreciation, an auditory medium becomes critical. Ask to sample the system before you sign up. Once you've seen the system, ask yourself how well you'll adapt to learning on it. For more details on delivery methods, see chapter 8.

6. Individualized Courses

Coast Telecourses' "Universe: The Infinite Frontier," described in chapter 2, comes with a video, a workbook, and a text. The materials are superb, but somewhere along the line a real teacher needs to facilitate the learning process for students. You want more from any program than what you can learn on your own. So be sure to ask these questions before you sign up for the course:

- How much of their expertise and personality have faculty members added to the course?

- Have faculty members gone the extra mile to make the learning experience positive?

- What special touch has the teacher added to make this course unique, not just "out of a box"?

- What leading-edge research or information has the professor brought to the course?

If you are taking courses taught at a university and transmitted to distance students, the question then becomes: Have the instructors individualized courses specifically for distance students? If so, how much? A lot can be done to make on-campus courses translate better for distance students. Extra-detailed course syllabi, clear course outlines, definite due dates, and super-clear assignments all in writing and given at the first class are the bare minimum for taking care of distance students' needs.

Now *This* is an Individualized Course!

Professor Charles Lyons, who teaches over a live one-way video, two-way audio system at the University of Maine, uses all manner of technology to individualize his courses for his distance students. He creates extra course materials, uses overheads specially created with distance students in mind, and even has students send in photographs of themselves. Lyons then puts the photos on a CD-ROM; when a distance student calls up to participate in a class discussion, Lyons can display a photo of him or her, so everyone in class can "see" each other. Lyons's students say this extra touch enables them to put a voice with a face, making them feel like they're an integral part of the class.

7. Student-Instructor Ratio

The theory "if you can't see them, it's less work" holds no water either for faculty or for students in distance ed. In fact, teachers report that distance ed classes take more of their time because the level of interaction is so much higher than in a traditional classroom.

You can assume that no matter what the medium, if there are consistently more than fifty students per distance class, you'll find yourself with a stressed and ineffective faculty member. For on-line courses (which are very time intensive), the ideal student range is low, about fifteen to twenty students per class. For other distance courses, the range can be a little higher.

One exception to the fifty-student rule is one-time seminars broadcast by satellite. Satellite seminars lasting a few hours typically enroll up to 400 students. This isn't a problem because seminars generally don't involve interaction.

F. Y. I.

LEARNING ON-LINE

An on-line course is one you can take by using your computer and modem to connect to a remote database or to the Internet. See chapters 6 and 8 for more information about on-line courses.

8. Peer-to-Peer and Student-to-Faculty Interaction

Most distance programs will provide you with a great deal of opportunity for interaction at all levels. But because you will be physically separated from faculty and fellow students, it makes sense to verify exactly how much of a commitment the institution makes to interaction.

Get specifics from the college. Find out exactly how many times per week the instructor is required to talk with students. What means does the college use to facilitate quick feedback between faculty and students—letters, e-mail, faxes, telephone? Do instructors have office hours just for distance students?

Also ask questions regarding student-to-student interaction. Will you meet other students in your distance classroom? Will you be involved in team projects that require you to work closely with another student? How will you communicate with other students? Who pays for the communication? In chapter 6 you'll find many examples of what life is really like in the virtual classroom, through the students' eyes. You'll see how important fast, consistent communication is to a good virtual college experience.

9. Residency Requirements

Before you sign up for a virtual college, be sure to ask about residency requirements. They can range from as little as one week to as much as six months or even a year. Occasionally, schools will waive the residency requirement if you can prove that you have access to the peers and equipment the school feels you need for a complete education. Get your waiver in writing. Make sure you won't be surprised by a residency requirement down the line.

10. Cost

Just as with a traditional program, you'll want to ask several key financial questions before you begin a virtual program. For distance students, the first thing to find out is whether the cost includes out-of-state tuition or not. Many distance programs do not charge out-of-state students extra. Others do, but they don't always let you know that up front. It's a nasty surprise when you discover that what looked like a great program is more expensive because you live outside the state.

Also, ask if there are extra charges for distance courses or materials. Few institutions charge extra for this, but those that do tend to charge anywhere from $20 to $140 extra per program.

And you'll want to ask about the availability of federal and state financial aid packages. Be sure to find out about the institution's loan default rate. If a school's default rate is too high, you may not be able to borrow as much money from the federal government as you had anticipated because of restrictions placed on the school. I explain this in detail in chapter 5.

11. Time to Completion

This is the question distance students most frequently forget to ask. It's really a two-tier question: How long does the entire program take to complete, and how long does an individual course take to complete? If you need your degree in two years, find a program that will let you accomplish your goal in that amount of time. But be reasonable. Distance ed programs are frequently designed to be taken on a part-time basis to allow you to continue with other activities while you pursue your education.

Some distance programs, particularly at the master's level, compress twelve-week courses into intensive five- to six-week courses. While it may sound great to progress through a degree program more quickly, students across the board report that compressed or intensive courses are extremely time consuming and require a lot of work. Three to four hours a day is the average amount of time distance students spend in such intensive courses.

At the other extreme, some programs allow as long as twelve months to complete a single course. Procrastinators report having trouble completing these drawn-out courses. If you tend to put things off, you may want to stick to courses that have more structure and allow less time for completion.

12. Transferability

Since some colleges will not accept transfer credits earned at a distance, the only way you can assure transferability of credits is to ask the college for written agreement to transfer in your distance credits. If a college will not agree to transfer credits ahead of time, in writing, you may find yourself having to repeat classes later.

Transferring distance credits may get easier in the future as more students attend virtual college. Many two-year colleges are having excellent success with the PBS *Going the Distance* program, and several four-year universities allow the Going the Distance program credits to be applied toward a four-year degree. (See Top Questions, near the back of the book, for more information on transferring credits.)

13. Transcripts

Some institutions, such as the Georgia Institute of Technology, offer distance students a degree that makes no distinction between credits earned at a distance and credits earned on campus. Other colleges do indicate on your permanent transcript that the credits you earned were via correspondence, home study, or distance study. If this is an important issue to you, ask the institution how your transcript credits will look.

14. Penalties for Withdrawal

If you enroll in a virtual college and then decide not to continue with the program before you have taken any classes, you should be able to get all or most of your money back. Get the school's withdrawal policy in writing before any money exchanges hands.

DANGER SIGNS

If you see any of these danger signs, be wary of pursuing a degree with the institution in question.

- **No accreditation.** Yes, some marvelous institutions are not accredited. But since you have a choice, stick with accredited institutions. It's safer in the long run.

- **Accreditation from an unapproved source.** I can't say it too many times: accreditation from an unapproved accreditor doesn't count! Do your homework, and check out the validity of the accrediting agency.

- **The institution will not let you talk to students or graduates.** If a school won't allow you to talk with students, walk away. Period.

- **The institution will not release student statistics to you.** Technically speaking, unless a school has made a claim about its graduates, it doesn't have to release student statistics to you. But if the school does boast about job placement, success stories, or anything related to how well students are doing, then you have the right to demand the statistical proof. If a school won't turn over that proof, it's a very bad sign. In fact, even if it doesn't make claims about its graduates, any reputable school will gladly give you statistical information about its students.

- **Attrition rate above 50 percent.** It is not uncommon for some distance programs to have dropout rates of 30 to 50 percent. Any higher, though, and you'd better start wondering why.

- **Reports on file with the Better Business Bureau, chamber of commerce, or consumer protection division of the state attorney general's office.** Here we run into a problem unique to distance students. Which BBB and which state's agency do you contact when you live in one state and the school is in another? Students can come from anywhere, so who's to know about student complaints? Well, it isn't easy. The best advice is to check the BBB and state agency of the home institution and of your home state.

- **For degree programs: scant library services.** If you're aiming for a degree, then you need the depth of knowledge and research skills that go along with that degree. Again, browsing around and pulling material from the Web may constitute a *part* of a library program, but if that's *all* you get, it's a danger sign.

TWO GREAT STUDENT-COLLEGE MATCHES

While it's important to emphasize all the elements you have to check out and pitfalls you should protect yourself from, remember that many fine virtual colleges do exist, and many satisfied students have benefited greatly from them. Here are two people who found good distance learning matches.

John Beagle

After he retired from the California Department of Correction, John decided that he wanted a more fulfilling job. His goal was to teach

STUDENTS' VIRTUAL COLLEGE CHECKLIST

Accreditation:

- Is the institution accredited by an approved accrediting agency? The United States Department of Education and CORPA, the Commission on Recognition of Postsecondary Accreditation, are the only two bodies qualified to approve accreditors.If you are taking a program for a professional degree, such as law or psychology, do you have in writing that the program is approved by the state you want to practice in? Check with the virtual college and with the state board granting approval.
- Have you checked for accreditation by the relevant professional accrediting association, if your degree warrants it?

Faculty:

- What training in teaching at a distance have the faculty members received?
- How frequently does the institution require faculty members to update their distance training?

Virtual student peer group:

- Where do the students in this program typically live? Do students come from a wide geographic range or a more narrow area?
- What is the age range of students and average age of students?
- What other diversity can you expect from the students at a particular institution?

Library:

- What specific library services are available to distance students?
- What library instruction is available?
- Is there a computer database available?
- How does the institution provide reference materials to students?
- How quickly are library materials provided?

Student services:

- Does the institution offer career and/or vocational counseling? educational testing and counseling? tutoring?
- What technical support system does the institution have in place? Is it free of charge? What is the response time? How often are technical support personnel available to distance students?

F. Y. I. — *(cont.)*

Technology:

- What specific methods are used to deliver courses?
- How well do the course delivery methods match the course materials?
- Do you like the course delivery method?
- Can you sample the course to see if you like the delivery method? Individualization of courses:
- Are distance courses individualized specifically for students at a distance? If so, how?

Student-instructor ratio:

- What is the average student-instructor ratio in the program or classes?
- What is the ratio in the specific class?
- What is the maximum limit to class size?

Residency:

- Is there a residency requirement to this program?
- Is the school willing to make exceptions to the requirement?

Interaction:

- How frequently do teachers contact students?
- How long is teacher response time to students' questions?
- Are class discussions and team projects an integral part of the course or program?
- How does the institution facilitate a peer network among students?

Cost:

- Does the advertised cost include out-of-state fees?
- How much have costs risen in the past five years?
- Are there any extra fees for distance learners? If so, what are they, and how often are the fees charged?
- What is the school's default rate on federal loans?

Timetable:

- How long will the program take to complete? What are the maximum and minimum completion times? Is there an average completion time?
- How long do individual courses last?

F. Y. I. — (cont.)

Flexibility:

- How much will this course or program bend to fit into your schedule and travel commitments?
- If the course won't bend, is the school willing to make any exceptions for you?

Transferability:

- Do you have information, in writing, about transferability of credits?

Transcripts:

- How are credits noted on your transcript? Is a distinction made for credits earned at a distance? What specific descriptive language does the school use?

Withdrawal:

- How long do you have to withdraw from a course without any penalty?
- What are the withdrawal procedures and penalties? Are they in line with state and federal guidelines?

General:

- Have you spoken with graduates of the program or institution?
- Do you have a feel for what the workload will be like?
- Do you know how many students have completed the program out of the number originally enrolled? If there is a high attrition rate, find out why.
- Have you comparison shopped? Try to find two or three other similar programs or courses. Compare cost, length of course, instructor-student ratio, and course goals.
- Have you checked out the program's claims? Schools are legally required to provide information to verify any claims about results. If you are taking the course for career or vocational placement, ask for the number of graduated students who are working in the fields the courses prepared them for. Ask to see surveys of student satisfaction. If this information is not available, move on—it's a danger sign.

math. But he lived in Porterville, California, a 1-hour commute from the nearest California State University campus. Fortunately for John, the California State University in Bakersfield has an extensive distance program via live satellite, a medium that suited him well. John is now only three courses away from finishing his bachelor's degree. While he had to make the long drive for a few of his courses, the majority came to him at a remote satellite site closer to his home. John says he got to have his cake (stay in Porterville) and eat it too (get his degree and change careers).

Barbara Gellman-Danley

When she became vice president of educational technology at Monroe Community College, one of Barbara's main tasks was to develop a distance learning and technology program. Though she knew all about broadcast, video, and audio technologies, Barbara was less knowledgeable about the newest computer technologies. She decided to give herself the edge she needed by becoming a distance education student herself—via computer-delivered courses. What better way to get on the inside track? Barbara enrolled in the New York University Virtual College program. From her home, she took interactive courses delivered entirely over ISDN lines and earned an advanced professional certificate in information technology.

According to Barbara, who has a long work day and young children at home, the Virtual College program was a convenient, albeit intensive, way to acquire the skills she needed to make informed policy decisions.

A STRATEGY FOR CHOOSING YOUR BEST PATH

The previous checklist was designed to help you weed out the good from the bad and narrow your focus to things that are important to you. If you are undecided about a college, go through the final checklist below. Think each step through, and write down your responses to each item. Don't hedge or sidestep any issue. This very practical, common-sense approach works well for me—perhaps it will help you, too.

1. Decide on your career and or educational goals. Write them down as clearly and as specifically as possible.
2. Decide what skills, educational programs, courses, or degrees will help you advance toward those goals.
3. Gather a list of available programs.
4. Narrow your list by automatically excluding any program that does not clearly help you meet your goals or meet your requirements.
5. Further narrow your list by rigorously checking the virtual college or program against the checklists in this chapter.
6. Make a new list of the remaining programs, courses, and colleges. Compare cost, interactivity, timing, and technology to determine which three institutions suit you best.
7. Apply to one to three colleges that meet your needs and pass the virtual student checklist test.
8. Depending on how many colleges accept you, further refine your choice and settle on just one college by weighing pros and cons.

(You'll find information about the application process in chapter 5.)

5

GETTING IN AND FINDING THE MONEY

READY, SET, GO!

Just about anyone can get enthusiastic about the idea of going to virtual college. But the twin worries of getting accepted to a good program and draining your personal financial resources can put a crimp on that enthusiasm. Instead of worrying, do a reality check. You have many options.

ADMISSIONS

The application and entrance process for distance education is basically the same as for a traditional college:

1. Request applications.
2. Gather transcripts, if required. (Transcripts are official records of classes you have attended and the grades you received for them.)
3. Take entrance tests, if required.
4. Request admissions and financial aid forms.
5. Complete and submit these forms.
6. Wait for schools' responses; if accepted, evaluate financial aid packages awarded. (For more information about financial aid, see page 73–83 in this chapter.)

Among distance ed institutions, you'll find two distinctly different application procedures: one short and streamlined, one longer and very much like those required of most traditional colleges. Fortunately, most virtual colleges only require the short application. You skip a lot of the traditional steps, such as taking entrance exams and gathering transcripts. Admission is simple, nonthreatening, and quick.

Let's look at the short and the long application procedures in more detail, so you know what to expect when you're ready to apply.

Simple Application Procedure

In a simple application procedure, you'll typically just fill out a short form and mail it in. You'll hear about admission relatively quickly, and you're pretty much assured of a spot. These short applications typically request your name, social security number, address, and a brief educational history. You're almost 100 percent guaranteed to be accepted; it's just a matter of giving the school the information it needs to get you in the system efficiently.

In most cases, you will not need to send transcripts or other proof of academic work for entrance. However, some schools will want to see a high school transcript if you've recently graduated from high school. More often than not, institutions waive entrance test requirements for adult students. But don't get the idea that this reflects the schools' low admission standards. What simplified admissions really reflect is the institutions' very good experiences with distance learners. (See chapter 7 for details on this point.) Also, institutions don't need to exclude students from admission due to physical constraints since distance learners aren't taking up physical space in a dorm or in an on-campus class.

You can expect the following types of distance programs to offer streamlined admission:

- community colleges (most)

- trade and vocational schools

- short certificate programs such as the Tax Training Institute mentioned in chapter 2

- single for-credit courses offered through universities' adult education or extension departments

- noncredit courses

- some degree programs (variable)

The Longer Road to Admission

Not all virtual colleges use a simple procedure, however. You'll typically find longer, more traditional admission procedures in place for more comprehensive programs leading to a degree or a certificate. That's because before making long-term commitments, institutions like to get to know students a little better than a short application procedure permits. You'll fill out a detailed application that includes your complete education history, you'll write an essay, and you'll often need to submit scores from entrance exams such as the SAT or ACT. Some schools will want the whole nine yards—the results of an entrance test, an essay, transcripts, and a detailed application. Others will just ask for transcripts and an essay, particularly from adult students. Your chances of acceptance will depend on how well you meet the program's entrance requirements and how many students the program accepts. You'll usually wait longer to hear about acceptance when you submit a formal application—anywhere from a few weeks to a few months.

Transcripts

If you are applying to a full four-year degree program, a master's, a Ph.D., or many of the longer certificate programs, you'll probably be asked to deliver some form of transcript along with your application. To do this, write or call every school where you have earned college credits and ask them to send you official transcripts. There may be a small fee for each transcript.

F.Y.I.

IMPROVING YOUR ACADEMIC RECORD

If you have a mediocre high school or college academic record, taking community college credits and single courses through the distance learning adult education departments of name universities is a great way to improve your GPA (grade point average). Then, when an institution next asks to see your official transcript, you can show the admissions officer a better picture of your real abilities.

What if you don't have any college credits to show on a transcript? As long as you're not applying to a graduate program, that shouldn't be a problem. If you are between 18 and 24 years old, send your high school transcript. And what if your high school days are long behind you? Again, no problem. The longer it's been since you graduated, the less inclined institutions will be to ask for your high school record. Schools figure you have gained work and life experience, which makes you a good candidate for admission no matter how you performed in high school. Schools have long experience with adult learners, and that experience is very favorable.

Entrance Exams

Very few distance ed institutions will ask you to take an entrance exam if you are older than 25. Some institutions, however, particularly those with an identical on-campus degree program, may expect you to meet the same requirements for admission that the on-campus students meet. That may translate to taking an entrance exam.

There are two levels of entrance exams: the kind you take to get into bachelor's programs and the kind you take to get into master's or Ph.D. programs. If you are an adult distance student, it is extremely

---

F.Y.I.

VIRTUAL APPLICATIONS

If you can go to college virtually, why not apply that way too? Using the World Wide Web and e-mail, you can do just that. So far a relatively small number of universities are set up to receive electronic applications, but you can expect most colleges to be wired within the next few years. But even when your favorite university does get wired, don't expect everything to be electronic—you still have to snail-mail your transcripts and application fee.

Jo Ellen Graham, director of graduate admissions at the University of California, Irvine, and one of the first experts to take the university application process on-line, says e-transcripts and payment technologies are being fine-tuned and will be available soon. Graham says between 8 to 20 percent of applicants are using the electronic system, with numbers increasing each year. To see an example of an electronic application, you can visit UCI's Web site (http://www.uci.edu/students/).

---

unlikely that you'll have to take the first level, the ACT or SAT. But if you do have to take one of those tests, don't be surprised when your more experienced perspective cuts those previously formidable exams down to a much smaller size. If you need to take an exam and you want to brush up, you can get coaching or take a class; you can also find a bevy of test-preparation books in your local bookstore.

In contrast to the rarely requested ACT or SAT, some graduate-level programs will ask you to take the GRE, or the GMAT for business school programs. Entrance to medical and law schools is another story; like traditional universities, virtual med schools require you to take the MCAT before you apply for admission, and law schools require the LSAT.

PAYING FOR VIRTUAL COLLEGE

You'll be glad to know that on average, a virtual education can end up costing you a lot less than an on-campus education. Some traditional expenses are eliminated right off the top. For one thing, you don't have to move or pay those high residence-hall fees. And many times, costs per credit hour are less than the on-campus equivalent.

If you have some work experience and previous college credits, your transfer credits and life experience stand to take a chunk out of the overall tuition bite. The less school you need to pay for, the better.

The total cost of your distance education will depend on what school you attend, the length of the program, what distance program you choose, and what transfer credit, CLEP, or other test-earned credit you can bring into the program.

To find out how much your schooling will cost, multiply the cost of tuition per credit hour by the number of credit hours the school requires for you to complete the credential, degree, or classes you want. This is your base number. Your calculations may change if you can take deductions for transfer or testing credits. But wait until the institution gives you notice in writing. Also, expect the cost of credits to rise about 10 percent per year; be sure to figure that into your calculations.

For instance, if you want to pursue a virtual master's degree at California State University, Dominguez Hills, you will need 30 semester credits to graduate. Each credit hour costs about $135; 135 ×

30 = $4050. If you take one year to complete the course, $4050 would be your estimated cost. If you plan to take two years, add $400 to your overall price to allow for probable tuition increases.

Distance Education Costs Compared to On-Campus Costs

As I've already mentioned, distance education frequently compares very favorably cost-wise to an on-campus education. The following chart will show you a cost comparison between on-campus course fees and distance course fees.

Cost of College Courses per Semester Credit, Distance Courses vs. On-Campus Courses

	Distance	On-Campus
Most Expensive		
Roosevelt University	$321	$321
Stephens College	$217	$400
University of Pittsburgh	$170	$579
Saint Joseph's College	$170	$190
Embry-Riddle Aero.	$140	$345
Least Expensive		
Mississippi State University	$ 50	$ 83
Chadron State College	$ 57.25	$ 72.25
Louisiana State University	$ 55	$260
SW Texas State University	$ 55	$102.33
Texas Tech University	$ 50	$ 82

Source: Independent Study Program Profiles, March 1996, National University Continuing Education Association, Division of Independent Study.

Special Distance Costs

You need to be very careful about "hidden costs" as a distance student. Be sure to ask about extra costs before you calculate your overall budget. On the next page is a list of the average maximum extra fees for distance education students. Some institutions charge none of these costs; others charge just one or two of them.

Study guide charge	$ 60
Telecommunications charge	$ 20
Transfer charge	$ 50
Nonresident charge	$800
(rarely levied, but always check)	
Mailing charge (books, library materials)	$ 35
Tapes, videocassettes	$ 25
Lessons	$ 26
Extension charge	$100

The Current Financial Aid Picture

There are four basic steps to getting financial aid for all students, traditional and virtual: determining need, finding appropriate sources of money, applying for aid, and waiting to see how much aid you're awarded (and when).

For virtual students, there's an extra step: determining if the program you want to pursue meets enough federal guidelines to allow you to receive all types of financial aid.

Step 1: Determining Need
The amount of tuition help you receive is based on formulas the United States Congress sets to determine your financial need. The formula you

Independent or Dependent?

If you meet any of the following criteria, you are automatically considered an independent student; otherwise, you are a dependent student.

- You were born before January 1, 1973.
- You are a veteran of the U.S. Armed Forces (Army, Navy, Marine Corps, or Coast Guard).
- You plan to enroll in a graduate or professional program (beyond a bachelor's degree).
- You are legally married on the date the application is signed.
- You are an orphan or ward of the court (or formerly a ward of the court, until age 18).
- You have legal dependents other than a spouse.

Source: United States Department of Education.

use to calculate your need is based on the category you fall into—independent or dependent student.

Step 2: Finding Appropriate Sources of Help

As a distance student, you may be able to receive aid from the following potential sources, depending on your need and the program you're enrolled in:

- federal government

- state government

- the institution you're attending

- private scholarships

- your place of employment

- the military (if you're enlisted or a veteran)

- miscellaneous forms of tuition help, like private loans and work-study programs

Note, however, that as a distance student, you may not have all sources of financial aid available to you, depending on the program you're enrolled in. Why? Just as Congress sets the formulas to determine your need, it also sets many of the laws governing which specific educational programs can receive federal assistance for students (and consequently, state and institutional aid for them). Again, because Congress is just now beginning the process of catching up to the current distance educational trends, distance programs must adhere to an exceedingly burdensome and archaic set of federal regulations in order to get federal financial aid for their distance students. Some programs work hard to adhere to the guidelines; others just say "forget it!"

Step 3: Applying for Financial Aid

As a distance student, you will apply for financial aid through your institution's financial aid office, probably via mail. The process tends to take longer than it does for traditional students, but other than that, everything else remains the same. You will still fill out a financial aid application and send everything to the financial aid office.

Each institution sets its own deadlines for applying for financial aid, so be sure to contact them for dates.

Step 4: Determining Program Acceptability for Federal Financial Assistance

Here is the area unique to distance students. A very complex set of laws determine which educational programs are eligible to give federal financial assistance to such students.

Rule: A semester needs to be fifteen weeks long. Congress likes programs to be in tidy semesters, with specific starting dates of classes and specific ending dates. This doesn't sit well with the philosophy of distance education, in which convenience and adaptability of courses are highly important.

Distance education considerations:

- No specific starting date on independent study classes poses a problem.

- Some programs finish before or after the fifteen weeks; again, a problem.

Rule: To receive a Stafford Loan (the most popular federal loan), students must be enrolled at least half-time.

Distance education considerations:

- Let's say half-time translates to a load of 6 credit hours. What if 3 of your credits come from a distance course that passes federal qualifications, and 3 of your credits come from a distance course that doesn't pass federal qualifications? According to current guidelines, you're not half-time, so you don't get the loan.

Rule: The institution does not qualify for federal aid if more than 50 percent of its courses are offered via telecommunications.

Distance education considerations:

- This rule does not reflect the direction in which distance education is going. Unfortunately, this rule already excludes dozens of great distance programs, and it stands to exclude hundreds more in the next five to seven years.

Step 5: Determining Payment Policy

You've applied for financial aid, but it hasn't arrived yet and now classes are beginning. What do you do? Do you pay for classes with funds of your own, or do you simply wait for your financial aid check to arrive?

What Kind and How Much Aid?

When you get serious about applying to a school, call the financial aid office and ask these questions:

- What federal aid is this program eligible for?
- What institutional aid do you offer apart from federal aid?

If the program is not eligible for any federal financial aid, perhaps the school has a great institutional aid package. If not, talk to the financial aid officer and determine if you can find alternative sources of funding. Many alternative sources exist, and financial aid officers are trained to help you find those sources. Use their knowledge!

Financial aid officers who work closely with distance students tell me that distance students' financial aid may be delayed slightly longer than that of on-campus students.

Interestingly, the biggest cause of delay is the computer software packages that colleges and institutions use to calculate students' financial aid budgets and needs, which are created with traditional students in mind. Frequently, when financial aid officers begin working with distance students, they have to begin calculating needs without aid of computer software, since several variables distance students bring to the equation aren't accounted for in these packages.

These hand calculations simply take more time, so processing your financial aid may, too. If you're counting on financial aid to pay all or part of your classes, ask how the institution will handle a delay in payment. Many simply wait until your financial aid arrives to ask for money from you. Others will require payment up front.

Who Pays?

Who pays for your education may depend on where you find yourself in the following categories.

High School Student

If you're a high school student, who pays for your education depends on whether you're enrolled in a public or private high school and what kinds of classes you're taking. If, for instance, you're taking courses at a distance because your public high school couldn't provide all the courses you need, then your high school will probably pick up the cost. Even if you're taking courses for personal enrichment, you may still be able to convince your public high school to pick up those costs.

At a private high school, you'll probably have to pick up all costs for extra high school classes.

If you're taking college-level courses while enrolled in public or private high school, you will need to pay for those courses. The best deal I know of is for high school students living in Bakersfield, California. These students, through the Young Scholars Program, can take up to two quarters' worth of college credit at the cost of $2 per ITV course. While not every institution offers such good breaks for high school students, be sure to ask if the college you're interested in does.

Corporate Employee

If you're a corporate employee, you may have the best deal of all. Many businesses and corporations offer tuition reimbursement programs to their employees. Depending on the tax laws in your state, corporations may be able to write off a significant portion of employee tuition costs—to the tune of about $5000 per year.

Full-time College Student

If you are a full-time virtual college student, it is unlikely you will have the time to work. Because of that, you will need to pay for your education with savings or find grants, scholarships, and loans or another source of money to see you through.

Nontraditional Student

If you are over 24 and attending virtual college part-time, then you may be in a good position to find an employer who will help you pay your education costs. If you can find one willing to allow you to work part-time and attend college part-time at the employer's expense, then it may be worth it to take longer to finish your degree. If you attend an eligible program at least part-time, you'll still be eligible for many forms of student aid, such as a Stafford Loan.

Military

If you're in the military, you have many excellent opportunities for tuition reimbursement. The current guidelines state that the military

Loans, Grants, Scholarships

A loan is something you have to repay, often with interest. A grant or scholarship is given to you outright, but frequently with a restriction or future obligation.

Federal Pell Grants are examples of outright gift grants—you owe nothing. But other grants and scholarships may require some form of service from you. For instance, someone who receives an academic scholarship for exceptional achievement in science may be required to participate in special research projects at the institution for the duration of that scholarship.

will give up to a 75 percent tuition reimbursement for your education. See the next section for more details.

SOURCES OF FINANCIAL AID FOR DISTANCE STUDENTS

As of yet, there aren't any special distance education scholarships or grants. (At least none that I have learned of.) Some distance programs do receive grant money, but the benefits are passed along in the form of lower costs, not money delivered directly to your bank account.

Nevertheless, as a distance student, you may qualify for numerous loans, scholarships, and grants simply by virtue of being a student. Among the many fine books on financial aid are the following:

Finding Money For College, John and Mariah Bear, Ten Speed Press (1996). This book may not be easy to find—you may need to special order it through your local bookstore. If you are serious about studying at a distance, it is well worth the effort, because it describes financial aid for nontraditional and distance students. To date, this is the only book dedicated to the nontraditional aspect of financial aid.

Peterson's College Money Handbook, Peterson's (1996). An extensive directory of financial aid programs offered by 1,600 colleges and universities, including need-based and merit-based scholarships. The software that comes with the book enables users to analyze their own financial needs and compare various aid packages. It's geared primarily toward traditional college students, but the basic information about applying for college aid will be helpful to all.

Peterson's Guide to Scholarships, Grants & Prizes 1997, Peterson's (1996). This 500-plus-page directory includes profiles of nearly 2,000 programs that give worthy students money for college. The accompanying software enables users to search profiled information in several categories and then print out a list of matching awards.

College Costs and Financial Aid Handbook, The College Board (1996). Like the Peterson's books, this one does not offer information especially for distance students, but it does provide standard information about your array of options. Its chief value lies in the extensive listings noting tuition costs, financial aid deadlines, grants and scholarships awarded, and total aid delivered for more than 3,000 colleges.

Funding Your Education, U.S. Department of Education. You can get this free booklet either in print or on the World Wide Web. You will find extensive information on all federal loans and grants. The print booklet is available through the Federal Student Aid Information Center, P.O. Box 84, Washington, DC 20044. For the booklet's Web location, please see On-Line Resources near the end of the book.

Need a Lift?, The American Legion Education Program. This remarkable little booklet gives information about scholarships for veterans and their dependents, but it is a good information source for scholarships and loans for all students. You can pick up a copy at your local American Legion Post or order it for $3 by writing to: Need a Lift?, P.O. Box 1050, Indianapolis, IN 46206.

Corporate Tuition Reimbursement

The bottom line here: ask or you won't receive. Not all corporations have tuition reimbursement, but many do. If you find that your employer doesn't offer it, negotiate to begin a program. If you're really serious about your education and already working full-time, then you might consider seeking out a new position with an employer who does have a tuition reimbursement plan.

Private Scholarships

There are two basic ways for you to find out about scholarships. You can ask your financial aid officers what software programs they have available for scholarship searches, or you can do the search yourself. If you want to do your own search, one of your best single sources of information about private-sector scholarships is the National Scholarship Research Service, which boasts the largest database of such scholarships currently available. When you send an application, along with a $75 fee to the service, your application information will be used to scour through a 200,000-plus database for scholarships matching your profile. A search takes about two to four weeks. The National Scholarship Research Service is a reliable source of information—it's been in business since 1979. Be warned, however, that mixed in with the good opportunities you may find some pretty bizarre and esoteric scholarships that aren't of much use to you. Still, it's worth trying.

> National Scholarship Research Service
> 2280 Airport Boulevard
> Santa Rosa, CA 95401
> 707-546-6777
> Average number of scholarships located: 20 to 25

You can also do a scholarship search with the free software that comes with *Peterson's Guide to Scholarships, Grants & Prizes 1997,* noted on page 79.

Private Loans

Many private lenders offer low-interest loans to students. Check with your local credit union or bank to see if it offers such a program.

Military Assistance

Tuition assistance comes in two forms for military personnel: tuition assistance for active personnel and the G.I. bill for veterans. If you are in the military, you can receive up to 75 percent reimbursement of your distance tuition. Of course, you must attend a VA-approved distance program. Also, you will need to meet minimum grade requirements to keep your reimbursement going. Contact your base education office for details on programs and benefits. Tuition assistance for active military personnel is separate from the G.I. bill, which comes into play after you leave military service.

If you are a veteran and you put money toward your G.I. bill while active in the military, when you attend a VA-approved distance education program the military branch you retired from will match your funds. The G.I. bill undergoes constant revision, so the amount of matching funds you receive will vary. For information on your education benefits as a veteran, contact the Veteran's Administration.

Veteran's Administration
810 Vermont Avenue, NW
Washington, DC 20420

Educational loans information:
800-326-8276

VA benefit information:
800-827-1000

Federal Government

The federal government is a rich source of financial aid. To apply for federal financial aid, you fill out a form called the Free Application for Federal Student Aid (FAFSA). You should always apply for federal aid as soon after January first of each year as you can. You can get the forms from your institution's financial aid office or from the address listed below.

I discuss only three of the most popular federal programs in this chapter; there are others as well. For more information, contact your institution's financial aid office or the U.S. Department of Education. (Note: Federal financial aid is almost always paid to your institution, so it's always easier to go through your school for forms, help, and filing.)

Federal Student Aid Information Center
P.O. Box 84
Washington, D.C. 20044
800-433-3243

Important: As a distance student, remember that you need to check your program's eligibility before you count on receiving any federal assistance.

Federal Stafford Loan

Federal Stafford Loans represent the biggest source of financial aid for students. Students must attend at least half-time to receive Stafford Loans and must be enrolled in an eligible program.

You can get either subsidized or unsubsidized Stafford Loans. Subsidized Stafford Loans are given out based on financial need. The government will pay the interest on the loan until you finish school. Unsubsidized Stafford Loans are not based on need, and interest begins accumulating immediately. You can choose among four repayment plans to pay off the loan.

The total debt you can accumulate is as follows (these numbers change from year to year, so be sure to check for the most recent information):

- dependent undergraduate: $23,000

- independent undergraduate: $46,000

- graduate student: $138,500 (including any Stafford Loans received for undergraduate study)

Federal Work-Study

The Federal Work-Study Program allows graduate and undergraduate students to earn money by working at their schools or at an off-campus nonprofit organization or public agency. Distance students can participate in Federal Work-Study, but it does take some extra effort to find and coordinate positions. Your financial aid officer can help you set up a work-study arrangement.

Federal Pell Grant

Students who have not earned a bachelor's or professional degree may qualify for a Pell Grant. There's not a lot of money in this pot, but what you get you don't have to repay. Pell Grants are based on financial need. The maximum Pell Grant for the 1995-1996 academic year was $2340.

FINANCIAL AID TIPS FOR DISTANCE STUDENTS

Margot Joy, associate's director of student financial aid at the University of Wyoming, offers the following tips for distance students seeking financial aid:

1. Don't try to figure out everything yourself. Ask a financial aid officer for help.
2. Ask about the kinds of aid available to you, and ask for help researching every avenue.
3. Be sure to ask when you will need to pay for your schooling and about deferred payment plans.
4. Make sure the program is what you want before you receive financial aid.
5. Before you commit to a program (and pay for it), make sure you feel you can complete it. If you drop out or don't get a passing grade, you will have to repay any loans you took out without having anything to show for it.

6

WHAT TO EXPECT IN THE VIRTUAL CLASSROOM

THE INSIDE STORY: WHAT THE JOURNEY'S REALLY LIKE

Tucked inside an old book in my parent's house is a photo of a 1952 presidential nominee, Adlai Stevenson. In the photo, Stevenson wears a toothy smile on his face, and he's resting his feet atop a ribbon-festooned platform. The clever photographer focused his camera not on Stevenson's face but on his feet.

There, worn into the bottom of the soles of his shoes, was the real story of what his campaign trail against Dwight D. Eisenhower was like: Stevenson had worn two gigantic holes into his shoe leather. Shoes don't lie. They shout all sorts of things about where their wearer has been walking and about how hard the trail has been. That's why, if you want to find out what a journey's going to be like before you begin it, you should ask those who've been on it, or walk a mile in their shoes.

In this chapter, you'll have the chance to walk in other distance students' shoes to get an idea of what their experience has been like. You'll see what kind of wear and tear virtual interaction, homework, research, tests, grading, and team projects exact. You'll also get a look at the dynamics that influence your comfort level—dynamics such as your learning style and how much time and energy you want to expend each day on the trail.

A Trek Through Three Virtual Classrooms

There is no such thing as a "typical" virtual classroom. How could there be? Due to the significant differences among the technologies used to deliver virtual courses, a virtual classroom simply cannot be described in one, two, or even half a dozen different ways. But let's look at three specific examples to get a sense of some of the virtual pathways you can take to the knowledge you want.

A Remote-Site Virtual Classroom

Rosemarie Roskom has almost completed her associate degree in management from the University of Maine. Because Rosemarie works a couple of part-time jobs, her virtual classes must fit snugly into her busy schedule.

For Rosemarie, going to class means driving 25 minutes to a remote site located about 50 miles from the main campus. There she walks into a classroom filled with television sets, telephones, and long tables lined with other distance students. She sits and waits for her live, two-way audio, one-way video class to begin. The TV monitors flicker on, and Rosemarie watches a live video image of the on-campus teacher in an on-campus class. Rosemarie can hear and see everything in the classroom as it happens. The teacher, in turn, can *hear* everything that happens at all the remote sites, thanks to the two-way audio, but can only *see* the live class because the video image transmits only from the class to the remote students.

According to Rosemarie, the best teachers incorporate the distance students into the class so seamlessly it's as if they're in the campus classroom. When Rosemarie has a question, she dials up the on-campus class on the telephone. She waits 2 to 3 minutes while her phone call is put through to the on-campus classroom. Then a bridge operator signals the on-campus teacher that a remote-site student has a question. (A bridge operator is a person who sets up a telephone connection that allows audioconferencing between two or more parties.) The instructor will address Rosemarie, then Rosemarie will go on the air with her question. All the students in all the class locations—on-campus and remote sites—will hear Rosemarie's question, but no one will see her on camera.

The class will continue in this manner for an hour. After class is dismissed, Rosemarie can access the University of Maine's library using computers at the remote site, she can study with peers in her remote class, or she can zoom off to begin her homework.

An On-Line Virtual Classroom

Kevin Kimma, the San Jose resident you met in chapter 3, attends class by going to his home computer, switching it on, and dialing into the University of Phoenix On-Line system with his modem. Kevin can connect to the system at any time of the day or night, as long as he attends class daily and keeps up with his assignments.

After Kevin logs onto the system, he reads the assignment the teacher has left, as well as feedback to a question Kevin asked yesterday. The instructor has asked for students to participate in a scholarly discussion of a specific topic, so Kevin reads the students' comments so far and begins to research the topic to add a comment of his own. He will spend anywhere from a half hour to an hour on the computer, then at least an hour off-line completing assignments.

Since Kevin has questions about a project, he e-mails three of his classmates to get feedback from them. He'll check back on the system in a few hours to see if their replies wait in his mailbox. Later, he'll do some library research on-line to get a head start on his term paper.

An Audioconference Virtual Classroom

A senior at the University of Wyoming, Wanda Sue Smith is just three semesters away from finishing her bachelor's degree in psychology. She lives in Moose, Wyoming, a mountainous, remote area that receives massive snowfall during all but five months of the year. Sometimes Wanda Sue snowmobiles in to take classes at a remote site in Jackson. But during the heart of winter, the deadly windchill factor and the shortened days keep her from getting to campus. So she goes to class by curling up by the fireplace with a notebook, her textbook, and a telephone equipped with a good speakerphone and a mute button.

When class time arrives, a bridge operator at the main campus calls Wanda Sue. The bridge operator connects Wanda Sue to the on-campus class and to the other remote students. Wanda Sue then listens on the speakerphone to a lecture along with the other students.

Usually, about twenty students are on-campus in a live class with the teacher, and other remote students like Wanda are scattered throughout sites in Wyoming.

When Wanda Sue has a question, she asks it. She can count on hearing all her virtual classmates' familiar voices during the course of the evening. After the audio portion of the class ends, she goes over to her videocassette player and watches a videotaped lesson in preparation for her next class session. She'll also read her textbook, write papers, and do research for several hours each day.

The Translation from On-Campus to Virtual

As you see in these examples, what you do in a course remains the same, but how you go about doing it has changed. We've all been in a traditional classroom, if not in college then in high school. You know the scenario. The first day of class, you grab the appropriate textbooks and notebooks and head to the classroom. Once in class, you get the course syllabus, look it over, and decide how much you're going to have to do to get a decent grade. You show up to class on a regular basis where you sit in a chair, listen, take notes, ask questions, and discuss issues. Sound familiar?

How much you discuss and interact in a traditional classroom depends a lot on the teacher. Some teachers drone on nonstop for an hour, allowing little time for questions or discussion. Others pop questions at you every 5 minutes, encouraging debate. After class, you return home, where you put in extra time on your own as you read the textbook, do homework, research papers, and study for tests. Eventually you take those tests, turn in those papers, and at long last, take the final exam. Along the way, you will have acquired new knowledge through your efforts.

Now, let's look at your virtual class. No matter how much technology enters the learning process, what you do remains the same as in a traditional classroom. In the virtual classroom, you still check out a syllabus, discuss the topic, read the text, do homework, attend class, research and write papers, take tests, and—most definitely—learn. But how you accomplish these tasks will change, sometimes dramatically, sometimes just a little.

In some virtual classes, you will need to attend at a specific, prearranged time with other students. The interaction will be live—in what is called "real time." In other classes, you won't have a set meeting time, and communication will occur asynchronously—that is, it will be delayed, as it is when you send a letter. Just as in on-campus classes, teachers vary widely in ability and the amount of interaction they want during class. All told, you'll find an array of personalities and knowledge coming at you, but in the virtual classroom it's coming at you in all sorts of different ways.

THE VIRTUAL CLASSROOM ENVIRONMENT

As you've seen, Rosemarie, Kevin, and Wanda Sue attend class in completely different ways. On the surface it may appear that their disparate virtual classroom experiences have no common ties whatsoever. But if you really look at their and others' virtual classroom experiences, you'll discover some important commonalities.

Interaction in the Virtual Classroom

You're not in the virtual classroom alone. First of all, in a virtual classroom you'll always have a teacher-facilitator to keep you on track, point out the pitfalls, and help you navigate odd twists and turns. You'll also have company from your fellow classmates, who will work with you in teams or on an individual basis.

Have you ever slinked into the classroom, slid into a chair, and left an hour later without having said a word? Well, you won't find that

---

F. Y. I.

BUILD YOUR PEER NETWORK

After you've settled comfortably into your school routine, remember to take the opportunity virtual college affords you to build a peer network. Plan, going in, to make the acquaintance of each one of your classmates—perhaps even to make a few friends. With that open attitude, you'll have good student peer support and perhaps graduate with a greatly expanded network of friends.

happening in your virtual classroom. Hiking along the virtual path is not a quiet walk. It's more like a lively tour with lots of talking, explaining, and networking going on at once.

Here's something that will blow away any isolation myths you may have been haboring about learning at a distance: whether you're taking courses on-line, through the mail, or via the telephone, you can expect to interact more in a virtual classroom than in a traditional classroom.

The reason is simple: instructors often can't see you, so they want to make sure you're with them and that you understand the lesson. Without the usual visual clues, such as eye contact, increased verbal communication is necessary. In fact, it's not unusual to find that distance teachers base at least 20 to 50 percent or more of virtual grades on class participation.

In the virtual classroom, you'll find increased verbal communication in the teacher-student relationship and in the student-to-student relationship. While chatting on-line or on the phone or over a satellite system may seem cold and remote, distance students most often report that they feel they are better able to communicate with peers and teachers in distance classes than in traditional ones.

Wanda Sue Smith says the audioconference environment is very intimate. "It's like having a one-on-one class with the instructor," she says. " I feel that I communicate much more in my distance classes than I do in my on-campus classes." Research backs up what she says. Because of the high interactivity, students don't report feeling lonely, debunking a common myth about learning at a distance.

In a major study of distance programs and students across the United States in 1993, the Western Cooperative for Educational Telecommunications gathered statistics about student-to-student interaction and student-to-teacher interaction in the distance classroom. The study, "New Pathways to A Degree: Technology Opens the College," reveals that the majority of distance students in virtual programs felt that "the quality of their interaction with instructors was *at least as good as, or even better than, the experiences they had in face-to-face classes.*" (Italics mine.)

Students rated audioconferencing, voice mail, and e-mail highest for communicating, with audio talk-back (in video courses) just below. On frequency of student-to-faculty interaction, students responded that e-mail afforded greater interaction than face-to-face classes. For communicating with peers, more than 80 percent of students who used e-mail said that the quality of their interaction with peers was unchanged or increased over their experience in on-campus classes. Audioconferencing also rated very high for enabling peer communication.

So if you're used to sitting at the back of the class and you're considering learning at a distance, be forewarned that you'll have a front-row seat in your virtual classroom. But don't worry if you've never been a highly communicative type. Students say that even though they are shy "in person," the fact that they're not face-to-face allows them greater freedom to come out of their shells to communicate.

It Takes Two: Tips for Positive Distance Interaction

The same advice holds true for positive distance interaction as it does for positive on-site interaction: be patient with others, and when there's a problem, try to bridge the gap by increasing communication.

F. Y. I.

WILL YOU SUFFER FROM THE "LONELY LEARNING BLUES"?

You may be surprised to hear that the majority of distance students, even though they are physically isolated from professors and other students, feel that they have all the connection they need to avoid loneliness while learning. In a survey of University of Maine distance students, 88 percent said they felt no need for more student-to-student interaction time in class. Even though you probably won't feel lonely while you learn, what if you fall into that other 12 percent of students who do want more interaction? Here are some recommendations from distance students and teachers:

- Use the phone to add a one-on-one personal element wherever you can to your classes. Call the teacher during office hours, ask questions, and ask for more interaction time with other students during class sessions.
- If you aren't currently communicating with other classmates privately, ask the instructor to set up a study team with you and one other suitable student. You can write letters, exchange e-mail, or talk on the phone with your distance study-buddy.
- If you are extremely isolated geographically, consider getting an Internet connection to allow you to communicate with many distance students and teachers from all over the world. (See On-Line Resources near the end of the book for information about this.)

Here are the specifics on how this works at a distance:

- If you're having trouble getting along with a teacher, try to meet the teacher in person. If you can't visit in person, talk on the phone. Try to make some kind of personal connection; attach a voice or a face to the name. Allow the teacher to get to know you. If you can't talk to or see him or her, write a letter and send a photo. Tell the teacher about yourself and what makes you tick.

- Think about how the statement will be perceived without your vocal inflection or body language. If the statement could be taken as ambiguous, add more descriptive phrases to make your meaning clear.

- Be patient with other people's spelling and grammar mistakes. Realize that students may be speaking English as a second or even third language. Also, remember that people who do not possess stellar linguistic skills may be spectacularly talented in other areas that aren't readily apparent to you.

- Do not publicly humiliate or correct another student under any circumstances. The fact that you can't see other students face-to-face doesn't change how they respond to public correction. If you really want to discuss an incident, a phone call or some form of private discussion will work best.

Yikes—A Virtual Spat!

Of course, no matter how much technology evolves, human nature remains the same. Spats and complaints do arise in virtual classrooms, just as they do in traditional classrooms. Spats in virtual classrooms seem

F.Y.I.

INTRODUCE YOURSELF TO YOUR PROFESSORS

It's never too early to get a dialogue going with your professors. As soon as you know which professors you'll be working with in your first courses, contact them. Just a simple, schmoozy "Hello, I'm your new student, and I'm looking forward to the class" will open the doors and set a good tone for your entire course.

to arise for slightly different reasons than they do in traditional classes. Most come from either a lack of patience with language skills or miscommunications due to lack of body-language signals.

Students in several on-line classes from completely different programs, for example, reported similar wars of words over spelling mistakes. A typical situation involved a student making a simple typo or spelling mistake and a classmate publicly correcting the mistake. The corrector then became a target of derision and acquired a reputation as being an arrogant know-it-all.

On the miscommunication front, the most frequent problems occurred when students (or teachers) said or wrote something that came across as harsh and overly blunt, such as a correction without a positive statement to soften the blow. Even a statement such as "Come on, you can do better" can be misinterpreted without the corresponding body language to help signal that it should be interpreted as an encouragement, not a put-down. When we correct each other in person, we can deliver a quick smile or a sympathetic look. Over the phone, on-line, or in writing, such corrections can come off as too hard edged.

Team Projects

The idea that two minds are better than one drives the assignment of team project work in the virtual classroom. Team projects also take advantage of the rich diversity available there.

When you're traveling along the virtual college path, partners who can show you different aspects of the trip can make the experience much more rewarding. You'll find team projects assigned most frequently in business and education-related degree programs, in which differences of background, work experience, and age serve as healthy tools to broaden students' outlooks. In the virtual classroom, team projects take more time to complete due to the complexity of communication. Most typically, team members collaborate via phone, fax, e-mail, and, occasionally, live on-line chats. Students report that it's very important to have a strong team leader to manage the communication traffic—and traffic jams.

The biggest communication barrier in the virtual classroom is time-zone snafus. Think about it: virtual classrooms can span the globe, creating potential time-zone differences among students ranging from as little as an hour to as long as an entire day. You can see how the simple task of setting a meeting time could become a tug-of-war.

The most important lesson for you as a virtual student team member is that when working on a team project, you'd better cure yourself of any procrastinating ways. You cannot wait until the last minute to work on team projects. Work must be paced consistently to avoid due-date crunches, or someone will be up at an unreasonable hour—and that someone may be you. Team members must agree on reasonable "meeting" times, do their share of the work on time, and try to communicate as much as possible, by e-mail and fax, ahead of time, to keep in-person meetings concise, on target, and productive. Setting an agenda for the meeting isn't a bad idea either.

Homework

Ah, homework. The word students love to hate. Homework in the virtual classroom, like homework in a traditional setting, takes place away from class, and virtual homework tends to look and function just like traditional homework. When taking English 101, you'll have to read the same poems and analyze the same short stories as you would in an on-campus English 101.

What's different in the virtual classroom, however, is that there's no teacher looking over your shoulder to urge you to complete your

---

Time Warp

Michael Triguboff, who lives in Australia, is completing an advanced professional certificate in information systems auditing from New York University via its ISDN-based on-line program. He has had an excellent learning experience, but he's had to make adjustments for time delays.

Consider what's involved: From New York to Australia is at least a 15-hour time difference, which skews due dates and the timing of team projects. According to Triguboff, everything works well as long as the team plans projects carefully in advance of deadlines. But if other team members wait until the last minute to complete team assignments, things aren't so easy. "I am operating on Australia time, and they are operating on New York time. If everyone wants to work on the project at 11 a.m., that's 2 a.m. *the next day* for me." Triguboff solved his deadline problems by working well ahead of due dates. When he is ahead, he ends up being right on time.

---

assignments. This may sound like an invitation to procrastinate, but you'd be surprised. Distance students are typically highly motivated, so they've devised ways of compensating for their weaknesses.

Almost all virtual students are very good at fitting homework into the nooks and crannies of tight schedules. Many report doing homework during the wee hours of the night when they can't sleep. They don't wait for the "perfect time" to do their homework; they grab whatever time comes their way and get going as quickly as they can.

Does studying at a distance mean that you need the discipline of Gandhi? Since distance students often study to earn a degree or get a better job, most find plenty of motivation to stick with it. But when pressed, each student I interviewed admitted that yes, you do have to discipline yourself to succeed and that without a teacher nagging, discipline does take more effort. Students say independent study courses require the most discipline, and courses with set meeting times and deadlines make self-discipline and self-pacing much easier.

Research

Your research needs as a virtual student will differ vastly depending on what kind of a program you're in. You may never need to research, or you may need to research constantly. If you're taking a single course on principles of accounting, for instance, your research needs will be far more limited than in, say, an anthropology course. The accounting course will be more self-contained; you'll probably only need a textbook and exercises to progress. But since long, meaty research papers are the mainstay of anthropology course assignments, you'll need to access extra books and articles on a wide variety of subjects.

How you'll get your hands on those extra books and materials will depend on where you live, the program you're in, and your proximity to one or more large academic or public libraries. It will also depend on whether you have access to a computer.

Now for the computer question: do you have to have one to research? Technically, no. But it sure helps. In fact, some colleges won't let you begin a distance program unless you have access to a computer. The longer and more complicated the virtual program, the more important it becomes for you to have access to a computer equipped with a modem.

F. Y. I.

STUDY TIPS FROM A VIRTUAL STUDENT

Cynthia Fyfe earned her associate degree in health information management from the University of Alaska at a distance. The entire time she was a student, Cynthia worked full-time in a busy hospital. She offered these helpful tips for students who worry about discipline. Her tips echo what other students and teachers recommended when I asked.

- Before the class ever starts, get organized. Have a notebook to organize your paperwork, and keep a section of your notebooks to log progress on short- and long-term assignments.
- Communicate with classmates frequently to keep up motivation. Cynthia recommends that students who are on-line communicate via e-mail.
- If you are attending class via audioconferencing or through some other means where you can be very relaxed, don't "go to class" in your pajamas or while you're in a reclined position. You'll be too tempted to doze off.
- Never, ever procrastinate research papers. You will not be able to get materials at the last minute. In your mind, get over the hump by separating that giant project into small tasks. Just do one small thing at a time.

Other oft-relayed tips from students include:

- Don't put off homework until you find a huge block of time. Fit your work into the small spaces in your schedule.
- Since starting homework is usually the hardest part, think to yourself, "I'll give it 5 minutes." Often, you'll be able to continue longer once you've gotten over the start barrier.

In chapter 7 I'll give you some suggestions about how to bring your equipment up to par on a shoestring. You'll be pleased to know how easily you can pick up a reliable computer for much less than the frightening sticker prices you see in computer stores.

Testing

As a distance student, you will be tested in one of three ways: you'll take tests under the watchful eye of a proctor, you'll take them by

---

F. Y. I.

RESEARCH TIPS FROM A VIRTUAL STUDENT

Robert Weldon, a distance student who lives about 130 miles from his home institution, the University of Maine, Augusta, can't just mosey over to a nearby library. The University of Maine is the nearby library. For him, researching in the virtual classroom means planning ahead.

To research, Robert scans the World Wide Web for general materials. He also uses his computer to access the University of Maine's library databases and catalog. Once he's found a book or journal he wants, he contacts the library and places his order, and his materials are sent out to him. It takes a few days for the materials to arrive. The system works well, as long as Robert has planned ahead. He says that no matter what type of virtual class you attend, waiting until the last minute to do your research just won't work.

---

calling in to a computer system, or you'll take essay or open-book tests. Most colleges and universities opt for the proctored exam. Students can go to a community college or a remote site, or in some situations the institution can designate a proctor. For example, your boss could conceivably function as your proctor if you took courses at your office.

When you take the exam depends on what kind of program you're taking. At Purdue, virtual students are required to take tests at the same time on-campus students take them. Purdue's distance students (who are always proctored for exams) fax the test in at the close of the class period. The instructor gets the test immediately and thus knows that the distance students have had the same amount of time to finish the test as the on-campus students.

In a typical correspondence course, on the other hand, you often take the test when you're ready to take it. You can take as long as you want, and you'll probably have an open-book test. Open-book tests are anything but simple. Both teachers and students say that open-book tests require more time and analysis because the tests are tough and very thorough. Essay questions, not multiple-choice questions, form the heart of the typical distance open-book exams.

Computer testing is another option you'll encounter in distance classrooms. In a computer test, you call a telephone number and read your multiple-choice or short answers into the phone. At the end of the

---

F. Y. I.

RESEARCH TIPS FROM A VIRTUAL LIBRARIAN

Karen Lange is the assistant director of extended library services at the University of Wyoming Libraries. She works extensively with distance students, from those taking a single course to those working toward an M.B.A. Karen says that virtual students at UW can fax, e-mail, or call in research questions. Reference librarians check every hour for reference requests from distance students and get back to them immediately. Librarians will also perform interlibrary loan requests for students who need hard-to-find materials.

According to Lange, distance students in the M.B.A. and nursing programs are required to have a computer and a modem so that UW can provide on-line library database resources for those students' more intensive research needs. Lange makes the following suggestions for students researching at a distance:

- Know your assignments well ahead of time. Request reference and research materials early on in the course to avoid any last-minute crunches.
- If you are in a panic about your research needs, call your school's reference librarian at the beginning of the course to ask for suggestions and help. He or she will help you choose research materials, select good search terms for your subject, and determine what resources are available.

---

call, the computer informs you of your score. The benefit of a computer testing system is that you get immediate feedback. The drawback is that it doesn't test depth or nuance of knowledge. Also, some students find computer testing intimidating.

The majority of college-level courses employ proctored exams. In contrast, according to a 1996 National University Continuing Education Association survey, 91 percent of all high school correspondence courses use computer testing.

Grading

If you think for a minute that virtual college translates to an easier walk when it comes to grading, think again. You can expect to do the same amount of work you would do in an on-campus course, plus you can expect to participate more than your on-campus peers. Distance professors typically employ a mix of written assignments, tests, and participation to assure a fair grade. Each teacher will use different percentages, based on what will help the students learn most.

Paul Wax, who teaches in an on-line environment through New York University's School of Continuing Education, says he bases 60 percent of students' grades on their level and quality of interaction. "The better students are on every night," he says. "I look for their total interaction in the course, on the database, with other students, and with me." Professor Wax also looks for high-quality, well-thought-out responses to questions and comments.

Jeffrey Klivans teaches at a distance at the University of Maine. He says that his distance students take the same exams and turn in the same papers as his on-campus students. He bases his grades heavily on exams and papers. Professor Klivans also requires his distance students to interact with him and with classmates as part of their grades. To assure interaction, he allows e-mail, faxes, postcards, phone calls, and notes on an electronic bulletin board, so no one is prevented from communicating because of a lack of technology. Klivans says that at the end of the semester, he is astonished at how much feedback he's gotten from his distance students.

FACTORS THAT SHAPE YOUR EXPERIENCE

Factors outside your control will subtly shape your virtual college experience. We talked about some of these built-in factors in chapter 4. We'll discuss two of those factors, course delivery and matching course content to delivery, in more detail now to see how they relate specifically to the virtual classroom.

When Getting There is Half the Battle (or the Fun): Course Delivery

You see a program you want. You check the quality and reputation of the home institution. You apply and you're accepted. You're ready to go. Then the first day of classes arrives, and you discover that you can't stand the way the course is arriving at your virtual classroom. Or worse, you like it, but you just can't figure out how to navigate through the technology.

Just as a pair of shoes impacts how comfortable your walk will be, course delivery impacts your virtual experience on every level. That's why, when you consider taking any distance education class, you should carefully examine the *manner* in which the course will arrive at your virtual classroom. And what may sound good in a catalog may not look or sound nearly as good in practice.

If you want to learn at a distance, *sample the system before you sign up*. If, after a sample foray into the course technology, you discover you don't have the skills to use the technology, decide whether you want to endure the learning curve. Perhaps getting yourself up to speed is worth the time and the effort, or perhaps you already know of another program with a more appropriate course delivery.

No matter what, if you feel even slightly lost or confused using the course technology, *ask for training before you begin classes*. Or move on to a program more suited to your style. Once classes start you'll be expected to learn and turn in work right away. If the technology gets in your way, you run the risk of falling behind and having to withdraw. If you withdraw, you may get the mistaken notion that you can't cut it academically, when the real issue is your unfamiliarity with the technology.

It's Not All a Bed of Roses

When Dr. Barbara Gellman-Danley signed up for her on-line virtual class, she didn't anticipate the steep learning curve she'd encounter when trying to attend her virtual classes. Barbara, who works as a professional educator and is very comfortable with technology, was already highly computer literate. She thought that learning the course delivery system would be a snap.

But the on-line classes she took used a nifty—and highly complex—Lotus Notes software package that allowed for delivery of text, graphics, and video clips. The bells-and-whistles software proved at first to be a real obstacle course for Barbara. Fortunately, she says, one of her classmates was an expert in Lotus Notes. "Ellen saw that I was floundering, and she spent hours helping me. She walked me through the system and got me on my feet," says Barbara. "From then on I was fine and enjoyed my classes."

Matching Course Content with Technology

The reason Cinderella fared so well with the handsome prince was that her foot fit perfectly into that fabled glass slipper. Likewise, your best virtual classroom experiences will occur when the subject matter you're studying corresponds perfectly with the technology used to bring it to you.

If, for example, you're taking a biology class at a distance, just talking about an amoeba won't help you nearly as much as talking about and seeing an amoeba. Thus, for a biology course, a visual medium needs to be incorporated into the course for the subject matter to really come alive for you. If you take a course in music appreciation, an auditory medium becomes critical. To really understand what a cello sounds like, you need to hear one being played.

I've listed obvious examples to prove a point. If you find yourself in a class in which the topic isn't matching the course delivery method, set an appointment with your professor to discuss your concerns. If you don't see any improvement, you may want to consider moving on.

Physical and Learning Challenges

By and large, distance education serves those with physical challenges and learning challenges very well. Students who are wheelchair bound,

---

Bach to Basics: A Course Well Matched to Delivery Method

Warren Burton, a music professor at the University of Utah, teaches a music appreciation course over the radio to hundreds of students each year. He has perfected the art of combining heavy-duty music instruction with lively, witty banter. The end result is a mix that fools you into thinking you're having fun, when you're really learning high-level music-listening skills.

Students fill out a response sheet as they're listening to the 1-hour broadcast. They can listen to the broadcast from home or even from their cars. Immediately after each radio class, students send in their sheets. This way, Burton can keep attendance and see how well each student is tracking with the course. If Burton sees that a student misses some beats, he picks up the phone and gets him or her back up to speed. At the conclusion of the course, students take the 50-question aural exams under the watchful ears and eyes of proctors at remote centers. Burton has had good results; even though his exam is tough, students have done well. Virtual college doesn't have to be fancy to work well.

Learning Styles in the Virtual Classroom

Play to your strong academic suit. If you're unsure of what that is, consider getting professionally tested to discover your learning style. Your local college or career center will offer the testing or refer you to someone who can help. The test you should ask for is called the Canfield Learning Style Instrument. If the college does not have the Canfield test available, simply ask for a learning style inventory test.

Once you know how you learn best, you can choose programs accordingly. If you do discover that perfect program, and you know it's delivered via a medium that doesn't suit your learning style best, you can ask the school offering the distance program for help in adapting your learning style to match the medium it's using.

for example, don't have to expend the energy to maneuver through a campus to class. But when physically challenged or learning challenged, choosing the best course delivery for you is perhaps the most important factor in assuring a good virtual experience. And you may have more limitations when trying to adapt the delivery method.

For instance, if you want to take a course by satellite and you are vision impaired, the providing institution will accommodate you in every reasonable way. This may include giving you large-print materials and perhaps an audiocassette and video backup of the visual materials presented over the satellite. But since the satellite medium is extremely visual, you might be better off choosing a less visual-dependent medium for your course delivery.

If, on the other hand, you are hearing impaired, the satellite medium may be the perfect answer for you. All you will need is closed captioning in order to benefit greatly from the highly visual satellite medium. (Most video courses are closed captioned.)

7

TIPS AND SKILLS FOR VIRTUAL SUCCESS

WHAT IT TAKES TO SUCCEED

If you ask almost anyone what it takes to succeed in traditional school, you'll get a variety of answers: good study skills, good reading ability, and so on. But if you ask almost anyone what it takes to succeed as a distance learner, you'll get blank looks with some interesting guesses. "Discipline?" or "Computer literacy?" are the most common. But neither discipline nor computer literacy sits as the cornerstone of virtual success. If you happen to be disciplined or computer literate, great. But if you're not, be assured that other attainable skills will help you become a virtual success story.

Student-to-Teacher Communication

If distance teachers had to pick one quality that differentiates successful distance learners from those who are unsuccessful, it would be "communication with the teacher." Over and over, distance teachers told me that the students who communicate right away with the teacher do the best in their classes. Teachers speculate that this is because personal communication makes the learning and the course "real" to the student. Instead of a name on a syllabus or a mere grade-giver, the teacher becomes a person who cares about your learning. When you connect with the teacher, you don't feel as though you're doing everything in isolation; what you're learning and accomplishing seems just as vital as it would if you studied on campus.

According to teachers, all it takes is that first phone call, e-mail, or fax to break the barriers and get a good experience. Communication can be as simple as "I watched the videotape, but I really didn't understand that last point you made" or as complex as a couple of paragraphs explaining a snag you've run into writing a research paper. Many distance teachers will take the first step, immediately introducing themselves personally to you. Reciprocate. If you're naturally shy, you'll enjoy the ability to communicate without face-to-face contact. There's just something magic about communicating with your professors from the start. Teachers say your ability to articulate your views about the classroom experience to them will pull you through the hard times and set you on the right course in your classes.

Efficiency

Another factor that makes for virtual success is efficiency. How good are you at getting a job done with a minimum of frills? At work, can you steer a course directly through a mountainous pile of paperwork yet still figure out how to get out of the office on time? If so, you're probably efficient. At home, do you get the chores done in an orderly fashion before moving on to special projects or some relaxation? If so, then you're most likely efficient. If you're not efficient, take heart: You can learn efficiency with a little practice. Teach yourself by giving yourself time limits for accomplishing tasks. Race the clock; always ask yourself, "How fast can I accomplish this task?"

Flexibility

Flexibility is very important in distance environments, more important than discipline. Perhaps being flexible helps because distance students have to reframe their approach to learning and studying, or perhaps it's because distance students simply have to bend and flex more as part of the distance learning process. Whatever the case, it seems that the more flexible you can be, the better you will do in your distance classes. If your heart races over every little surprise in your schedule, you may need to work on your flexibility if you want to be as effective as possible.

Ability to Balance a Schedule

Most distance students have busy schedules filled with demands on their time. Children, spouses, jobs, and hobbies barely leave time for school.

As a distance learner, you probably won't be able to afford the luxury of hours upon hours of uninterrupted time to study and immerse yourself in library stacks. You'll need to fit your study in between doctor's appointments, jobs, and your kid's soccer practice. If you can usually find the time for all that's important, or you think you can learn how, then you're a good candidate for distance learning.

Resourcefulness

Are you good at finding ways of getting around problems? That resourcefulness will stand you in good stead in your distance endeavors. In talking with many students and teachers, I've found that most distance students have to "wing it" sooner or later. Instead of having an entire library at their disposal, for example, they may only have a bookstore and a small public library. But that local bookstore and library can become Grand Central Stations of activity for ordering and borrowing books.

Persistence

If you decide before you begin a distance program that you're going to stick it out no matter what, chances are that you will. If you already know you're going to finish a course, then communicating with teachers frequently, completing homework, and disciplining yourself to study when you're tired will come much more easily. It's not a matter of "will I?" but "how well will I?" This one simple mind-set change really makes a difference.

Techno-Skills

Obtaining tools for the future is a simple task with big payoffs. In fact, it's a lot like learning how to drive a car: the payoff is tremendous mobility.

Computer Literacy

If you know how to turn on a computer, copy disks and files, and use a word processing program, you're well on the way to computer literacy. Now, add on-line skills to your basic knowledge. Learn how to use a modem, go on-line, and get cozy with sending e-mail. If you can do these things, you're already in great shape. If you can't, it will be well worth your time and effort to learn.

F. Y. I.

FOR THE TRULY TECHNOPHOBIC

Ask for specific help from the institution you're attending. Don't be embarrassed. Even if it's "just" a videocassette player that gives you trouble, find someone who can help you. Let the school help get you comfortable using whatever tools you need to take classes. If you're really afraid of a computer, start by learning in unlikely but friendly places. Use what I call the "game plan": sit down with a great computer game. Don't scoff! Entertainment software is often the most user-friendly and advanced software on the market today. It's a lot more fun to play 3-D, interactive chess or solitaire on a computer than to point and click through some computer tutorial. You'll find you'll be able to become friendly with a computer faster by having fun first.

Hypertext Literacy

Hypertext literacy means you have specific skills in understanding and effectively learning from hypertext documents (see box).

You should care about hypertext literacy because of the World Wide Web's increasingly critical role as a mass communications vehicle. The Web is composed of many interlinked hypertext documents. That by itself makes hypertext literacy a critically important skill.

But there's one more reason to get hypertext literate: There's a strong possibility that many books we use in the very near future—particularly textbooks—will be hyperbooks.

Researchers Lynne Anderson-Inman and her associate Mark Horney at the Center for Electronic Studying at the University of Oregon caution that hypertext books may not be effective tools for all learners because they demand special skills:

- **Knowledge of a document's structure (big picture skills).** Before reading a hypertext book, it helps to take a broad, big-picture view of the document's structure. Know the material's length (short story, novel, chapter of a textbook, or short article?). Also, since hyperbooks and the Web aren't always organized like traditional books, it's important to understand how the material is broken up (by chapter or idea, plot segment or subject matter?) Figure out the overall structure before you begin reading, and you'll be one big step ahead.

106

Hypertext and Hyperbooks

Hypertext is a way of linking concepts in an electronic document. The links can lead to more text, a movie clip, a sound bite, an animation, or a graphic.

By way of example, let's say the following sentence is in a hypertext document: "Henry Purcell wrote the Pavane in A minor in the late seventeenth century." Each underlined word is hypertext. Were you to click with a mouse on "Henry Purcell," you would go to a new page containing Purcell's biography; were you to click on "Pavane in A minor," you would hear a sound clip.

Hyperbooks are book-length documents composed of hypertext. Because of the influence of hypertext, hyperbooks are organized differently than standard books. For example, if the book you're holding now were a hyperbook, this definition would have been accessible by clicking on the word "hyperbook."

- **Sense of purpose when using hypertext.** For those who have a wandering mind when reading, hyperbooks and hypertext in general greatly enhance your ability to roam. Hyperbooks and the Web aren't linear, so wandering is built in. This could be a drawback. To make sure it isn't, before you sit down to use the Web or a hyperbook, write down your learning goals and stick to them. If you're supposed to be learning about the Civil War, stick to that topic and that alone. Don't run off after every single sound bite, video clip, and graphic just because they're available. Chase too many links to extra information and you'll learn very little; you'll distract yourself from your main task.

- **A multiphasic (several times through) approach to reading.** When reading hypertext, once through is not always enough. According to Anderson-Inman and Horney, you should revisit pages you've already read to review information you may have overlooked the first time. This seems obvious, but people using hyperbooks have a tendency not to revisit pages unless the books are specifically set up to encourage revisiting and reviewing. This same reading pattern may also apply to using the Web.

Information Literacy

Information literacy used to mean we knew how and where to find the information we wanted. It was a lot like digging for hidden nuggets of gold. We don't have to dig for information anymore; what's more likely is that we have to dig out from under too much of it.

Start your information literacy campaign now by learning how to choose among print, television, videos, CDs, CD-ROMs, and the Internet and Web for information. Always ask yourself: Where else could I find this fact or statistic? Which medium translates or holds this information best? Sometimes print is best; other times CD-ROMs will be superior.

Think for a moment of a nonacademic example: video guides. You can buy a giant, 1,000-page video guide, or you can buy a CD-ROM containing the same video guide. I vote for the CD-ROM. Why? You get video clips, and you can search the videos with your specific criteria in mind. A CD-ROM is simply more efficient for wading through the morass of videos available. And with a CD-ROM you won't have to read tiny print like you find in those big guides.

Phase two of your information literacy campaign begins when you get your information. Expect to get too much. As with hypertext, stick to your goal and ignore the data you don't need. Filter. Give up those scintillating but useless facts; that extra information is mind clutter. Don't let it in to begin with, unless you're intentionally browsing for ideas, not answers. To stick with our example of a video guide, if you use a CD-ROM, you won't want to spend hours watching every movie clip just because they're there. Use them only as information, not as entertainment.

Phase three of your information literacy campaign comes when you evaluate the quality of the data you receive. Electronic data are inherently better or more accurate. When dealing with subjects for serious study, always try to verify your facts in two media. For instance, if you see a statistic on the Web, make a phone call to verify it, or send an e-mail message requesting a printed brochure verifying it.

Electro-Schmooze

You know how to charm people face-to-face; perhaps you even can transmit your charm over the phone lines. Now discover the other ways you can transmit your personality across a distance. I call this electro-schmoozing. The main vehicles for electro-schmoozing are e-mail, on-line chatting, bulletin boards, MOOs, and, of course, on-line classes.

While you may chuckle to yourself about this concept, it's going to make a big difference in your future effectiveness. For instance, e-mail is already a standard business and learning tool; you can expect even more reliance on e-mail and other electronic communication in the very near future.

Some people have already become experts at e-schmoozing. You can become good at it too, simply by noticing exactly what you like about the e-mail that you get that you respond positively to. Over time, you'll collect a repertoire of ideas about e-communication. You'll know instinctively what works and what doesn't.

Tips from Distance Teachers

Here are important pointers for distance learner success that I've rounded up from experienced distance teachers. Each has experience with a slightly different type of virtual classroom, as well as different geographical and subject areas. As you read the teachers' tips, you may be struck by how much value they place on early communication in a course. Quick and continual communication is a strong indicator that someone will be successful in a course. These teachers also noted two other important success factors: flexibility and consistency.

Paul Wax, professor, recipient of New York University's 1996 Teaching Excellence Award; teaches technical computer systems via on-line computer conferencing:

- Set a routine and stick with it. If you work during the day, set a time every evening when you will attend your virtual class.

- Communicate with your classmates and instructors early in the course. Don't wait; sign in or log on the very first day of classes and get a peek at what's happening. If you wait too long, you'll be behind before you know it. Also, the more you communicate with your professor, the more your professor will respond, and the more benefit you will get from your course.

- If the institution offers preclass training, take advantage of it! NYU offers training sessions for the on-line learning environment, but unfortunately, not all students show up for it. Later on, many of those students have a learning curve to overcome and have to get training as they keep up with the course.

Jane Granskog, professor, California State University, Bakersfield; teaches anthropology via live ITV:

- Find a vehicle for communication with the instructor that you feel comfortable with. Use it frequently to ask questions and clarify your ideas.

- Set deadlines for yourself, even if the teacher doesn't set any for you.

- If you feel tempted to "blow off" a homework assignment or project (or even your own self-set deadlines), remember that the benefits of what you're doing outweigh the temporary discomfort of any homework or studying you need to do.

Charles Lyons, professor, University of Southern Maine; teaches graduate-level education via live one-way video, two-way audio:

- Be flexible; we're on the frontier of distance education, so expect a few bumps in the ride from time to time. Take them with humor and an adventuresome spirit.

- At least once a week, and daily if possible, communicate with your distance professors. Extra communication will personalize your learning and really help keep you on target and motivated. If you don't have e-mail, use the fax machine. If you don't have a fax machine at home, find one in a neighborhood grocery store or copy center.

Cheryl Burnett, professor, University of Wyoming; teaches law and administration of justice via audioconferencing, pretaped video:

- Preparation before class is crucial. Because distance learning is so participation intensive, you need to have something meaningful to contribute to class discussions and projects. Don't expect to coast in a distance class.

- Be prepared to invest time every day in your class. Approach your class just as formally as if you were going to an on-campus course.

- Create a one-on-one dialogue with your teacher immediately. Call the teacher and ask questions regularly; exchange ideas about the subject matter. The sooner and the more frequently you communicate, the better.

John Hulpke, chair, Department of Management, California State University, Bakersfield; teaches management and business via ITV:

- Don't skip the daily practice exercises just because you think you can get away with it.

- Use "stealth" learning techniques to your advantage. If you can privately replay or review a class you've seen live by using videocassette or audiotape, make the extra effort to do so. You will dramatically increase your learning, particularly if you prefer to learn without distractions.

- Don't let your energy level drop because you're not in a live setting. In your mind, make whatever distance learning environment you're in as energetic and as important as a "regular" class.

TIPS FOR BRINGING YOUR EQUIPMENT UP TO PAR

Before you panic about purchasing the technological tools to learn at a distance, check to see what you really need, as well as what the school will provide. You may be pleasantly surprised. Most distance students think they need more than they really do when they first start out.

While it's fun to stock up on school tools, your supplies can be a whole lot more expensive than a pack of pencils, so be circumspect before you go on a shopping spree. Here are some tips.

General Equipment Tips

- Perhaps the school will have the resources to provide your equipment for you, from phones to VCRs. Your first order of business is to ask.

- If you must purchase equipment, such as a phone with a speaker or a VCR, ask for the phone numbers of former students. Call and talk to them. They may be a good source of recommendations for the best-working equipment and the best deals.

- Don't be afraid to buy used equipment. Go to secondhand office supply stores and scout the classifieds.

- If you must purchase some equipment, bargain hunt. Do you really need to spend $200 extra dollars on features you don't require for effective distance learning?

Computer Tips

Now that you're thinking about that great computer-delivered distance education program, you may be looking for ways to cut costs on purchasing a computer that will do the job. Here are some suggestions on how you can find the best deal.

- If you work at a business or corporation, check with the human resources department and see if it offers computer purchase loans. Many corporations offer no-interest loans up to about $2000 for the purchase of a computer. The loans can be paid back by payroll deduction, usually over the course of two years. If your employer doesn't have a computer purchase loan, find out if it will institute one. Or if the company's upgrading an employee's computer, it may be willing to sell you the old one.

- Computer clubs and societies regularly offer members and students low-cost used equipment. I know of several people who have purchased perfectly suitable computers for under $500 this way. Remember, computer club members probably want the very latest equipment. What they cast off as "ancient" may be less than a year old!

- Ask the institution you're attending if it has special loans or grants for purchasing equipment necessary for the program; this isn't at all uncommon.

8

A WORLD OF DISTANCE LEARNING METHODS

THE CURRENT TECHNOLOGY OPTIONS

Current options in distance education are vast; in this chapter you'll read about the ones you're most likely to come across on your virtual journey. Keep in mind as you read that it is very unusual to find a technology used in isolation today. Distance ed has grown into a community of distance resources, and virtual programs use anywhere from two to five of them. One technology will deliver classes, another will support those classes, and others will help students communicate with teachers and in groups.

For many sophisticated delivery methods, the institution will supply all the expensive equipment. Your costs, no matter what technology you use, will be reflected in your price per credit hour and in surcharges. The question of additional charges for use of technology is one that you'll want to be very specific about when you discuss costs with an institution. (See chapter 5 for a list of the most common extra charges.)

Print

Print was the first distance ed technology to arrive on the scene, and today it's as important as ever. In fact, print forms the base of them all.

F. Y. I.

HOW DISTANCE TECHNOLOGY MEDIUMS
ARE USED TODAY

While all the technologies coexist in today's virtual college, it is the video technologies that reign supreme, at least in U.S. distance education. (In other countries, radio and audiocassettes are most popular.) Video is always bolstered by a base of print and audio technologies. E-mail and faxes frequently facilitate fast communication.

In the U.S., the most common combinations are:

- Video materials + audioconference + print + e-mail and fax
- Audioconference + print + e-mail and fax
- On-line computer network and database + print + telephone and fax
- Print + e-mail + videocassette, audiocassette + telephone and fax

---

No matter how your particular virtual classroom is set up, all distance courses include a print component.

The main forms of printed material you will find include prewritten, printed course materials and independent course materials. Printed course materials include workbooks, study guides, and texts carefully designed to work seamlessly with other distance components such as videocassettes, audiocassettes, or teleconference sessions.

Independent course materials include all of the articles, newspapers, and texts the professor or the student collects and includes as part of the course. For example, a professor may require students to read the *Wall Street Journal* for business information or may collect a group of articles that supplement other course materials.

Recently, instructors have been placing print materials on the World Wide Web for students to access via computer and modem. That way, instructors can add or subtract print materials as needed. This is print "wired," but in essence is still just print. The advantage of wired print is timeliness: students have no wait time for the mail. The disadvantage is that students may still want to have a print copy of materials and may wind up printing out copies on their computer's printer. Paper and ink costs can add up.

Print is particularly useful for communicating specific, factual information. Almost all courses benefit from some print component.

Audio Teleconferencing

Audio teleconferencing, a very popular medium, uses telephone lines to connect two or more people at once. An operator sets up what is called an audio bridge to connect the parties together on one line, like a party line. The bridge is most typically provided by the institution sponsoring the course.

Audioconferences work very effectively in distance education for most kinds of classes. Live, two-way audio allows students to establish a rapport with the instructor, ask questions and receive immediate feedback, get support, and establish a good pace of instruction. (Print-only distance ed differs in that you must set your own pace of instruction.) Pure audioconferencing is obviously unsuited to courses requiring hands-on lab work or work with machines or tools.

As a note, students across the board rate this medium very high in terms of effectiveness and in how much they enjoyed using it.

Radio

Virtual colleges create a radio classroom by sending radio signals either live or from a prerecorded program. Anyone with a portable radio within the delivery distance of the station can receive the signal. Despite radio's easy accessibility and low cost, few radio applications for distance ed exist in the United States. Radio is, however, very popular overseas, particularly in developing countries.

Radio is best suited to nonvisually dependent classes, such as music appreciation, psychology, and other highly verbal or auditory subjects. You'll often find radio used in conjunction with print and e-mail technologies.

Audiocassettes

Audiocassettes are prerecorded tapes of instruction. To play them, you will need a cassette player. You'll find audiocassettes used most frequently when there are a small number of students enrolled in a particular class. The small class size does not justify paying broadcast costs; thus, audiocassettes are used. (In Europe, in the Open University in Britain, audiocassettes combined with print material are often the first choice for distance course delivery.)

Audiographic Teleconferencing

Audiographics is a type of audio-based technology that uses simple phone lines to transmit visual information such as drawings and charts. Specifically, audiographics uses narrow band telecommunication channels to transmit visual and voice images over telephone lines. A facsimile (fax) machine is a simple example of this kind of technology. Audiographics is most frequently used when visual images are integral to the instruction. Mathematics, engineering, and art are examples of such courses; each requires nontextual written information as part of the subject matter. (Imagine how much time would be wasted using spoken words instead of images to show calculus equations.)

Other examples of common forms of audiographics are electronic blackboards, telewriters, electronic pens, slow scan video, and compressed video. (Please read the definitions of the technology below if you're unsure of the terms.) If you're taking any course that requires a great deal of written interaction, such as art, science, mathematics, and certain languages, audiographics are valuable tools.

Electronic blackboards transmit images of anything written on the blackboard to television monitors at remote sites. For example, a teacher will write a formula on an electronic blackboard. A telephone line will pick up the signals from the pressure-sensitive board, then send them to a monitor at a remote site. Most frequently, colleges use electronic blackboards in conjunction with audio teleconferencing in math and science subjects.

Telewriters and electronic pens are computer-based systems that allow remote learners to see anything drawn or noted on a special tablet. If you're learning Chinese, for instance, and you write the highly visual characters on a special graphics tablet with an electronic pen, the signals will be coded into sounds and transmitted over a phone line to the teacher. The teacher can then visually check your characters and use a second phone line to discuss the characters with you.

Fax machines allow students and teachers to transmit documents containing text and graphics over phone lines. Students and teachers can also use computers equipped with combination fax/modems to send text and graphic material over phone lines right from their word processing programs or computer graphics programs. The images will be transmitted in black and white. A fax takes about 30 to 60 seconds to arrive at the receiving fax machine.

F. Y. I.

STUDENTS' FAVORITE DISTANCE TECHNOLOGIES

When I talked with distance students, several technologies stood out as very positive: audioconferencing, on-line programs, e-mail, videotapes, and faxes. The more varieties of technologies used in the virtual classroom, the more the students felt they were able to communicate and learn.

My anecdotal evidence cannot be taken as a formal study. Here are, however, some percentages from a formal study about students' likes and dislikes. The study corresponds closely with what I discovered in talking with distance students. (Audio talk-back, by the way, refers to videoconferencing with a two-way audio system. See the section on video earlier in this chapter for details on this type of system.)

Technology	High Positive	OK	Negative
Computer Programs	90%	10%	0%
E-mail	74%	21%	0%
Audio Talk-back	57%	37%	6%
Voice Mail	39%	62%	0%
Audio Conferencing	60%	37%	4%

Source: WICHE New Pathways, 1994.

Slow scan or freeze-frame video transmits one frame of video at a time over a telephone line. The intervals between each new frame range from 30 to 60 seconds. Freeze-frame video costs much less than full-motion video. You'll most frequently find freeze-frame video used in two-way audioconference virtual classrooms.

Instructors use the video images to deliver illustrations, photographs, models, and other visual images. This technology is not used to "tape" a teacher giving a lecture. (If you find a course claiming that it *is* used for this purpose, run the other way.) It's best used for electronic slide shows that illustrate points the instructor is making over a live audioconference.

Compressed video allows video signals to run via telephone circuits. Since video contains a great deal of information, the video signal is reduced and squeezed before it's sent. A single transponder on a satellite can also transmit compressed video. The great difficulty with compressed video is that any rapid movement looks very jerky. This is because when compressing the image, some of the "information" is removed, creating less-than-whole frames. Students taking classes via compressed video report that its quality is frequently poor and can be distracting. It takes some time to get used to it.

Video

Video enjoys enormous popularity in distance programs. As a distance student, you will probably encounter some form of the video medium in your virtual education. It's easy to understand why video is so popular. Video allows students to perceive nuance, body language, personal interaction, and movement as only a live view of a situation could afford. It's the "next best thing," as long as it's used correctly. (But other technologies also do a wonderful job, and some surpass video, depending on subject matter.)

Many types of technology can deliver video images. Video information can be transmitted live via radio frequencies, telephone lines, coaxial cable, fiber optic lines, satellite, and microwave. Video can also be prerecorded and broadcast as instructional television via those same methods. Or video can be recorded onto a videocassette and mailed to students for viewing in a videocassette player.

Videoconferencing

You may not realize it, but you've probably seen a videoconference. When you see news anchors broadcasting live from an exotic foreign country, clutching their microphones and speaking to the viewers at home, you're seeing a one-way video, two-way audio videoconference.

Videoconferencing refers to a real-time session in which full-motion, full-color systems send one- or two-way signals through

---

F. Y. I.

REAL TIME

Real time means you see or hear things as they are happening. You don't experience any delay. A phone call is in real time; a letter you mail is not.

F. Y. I.

INSTRUCTIONAL TELEVISION (ITV)

Instructional television consists of live or pretaped programs that are broadcast over open-circuit channels operated by the Public Broadcasting Service public television stations. All you need to receive ITV is a television set.

---

satellite, fiber optic, or coaxial lines. Some of the newest videoconferencing technology allows for full-motion videoconferencing over ISDN lines using a computer.

The audio portion of a videoconference is transmitted via telephone lines or, in some instances, via satellite. The most frequent configuration is for video transmission over satellite and audio transmission over phone lines. Satellite technology is best employed for transmitting information over very broad geographical areas. Satellites can broadcast ITV, live instruction, or pretaped telecourses.

Other ways of transmitting video include the following:

ITFS Instructional Fixed TV Service uses microwave transmission to broadcast signals over about a 25-mile radius. A low-cost antenna at a receive site collects the microwaved signal and converts it to a television signal. (Signals can also arrive via satellite or cable.)

Because of the special equipment needed, schools and institutions set up remote sites where students can meet to view the transmissions. The ITFS option is employed most frequently in local or regional virtual programs to deliver one-way video with two-way audio.

CATV Cable Television uses fiber-optic or coaxial cable lines to deliver one- or two-way signals. Cable can transmit directly into your home if you live close enough to allow cable hookup. This expands student flexibility.

Videoconferencing can involve either a one-way or two-way video system. Two-way video is extremely expensive to operate, so you'll rarely find this option used in distance ed. The most typical configuration will be one-way video, two-way audio, with the audio coming over telephone lines. If you do find a two-way video system, it will more than likely be for local broadcast only, not national. When video is broadcast to more than one receive site, it becomes increasingly expensive. Also, it's difficult to allow for two-way video because of classroom semantics. Each site has a separate monitor—just imagine a single professor trying to keep track of 100 monitors, each showing a roomful of people. While you're looking at the image of one professor, he or she is being visually overwhelmed by the number of receive sites.

Videoconferencing is most useful for teaching subjects in which a video and an audio component are musts. Nursing skills, for instance, often require full-motion demonstrations with a live explanation for fully effective teaching.

Videocassettes

A videocassette holds taped information conveying full-motion video and audio. The beauty of a videocassette is that it allows you great flexibility. You don't have to go to a receive site to watch it, and you can review it as many times as you want, whenever you want. Many distance programs combine videotaped lessons with live audioconferencing. Thus students can benefit from a visual component and from the immediacy of the live audio component.

You'll find that videocassettes are a widely used distance ed option. Students like videocassettes because they get to see visual information, yet they maintain the scheduling flexibility they want. Videocassettes are best used for courses requiring a visual component to teach the subject. For example, a distance course about courtroom practices would benefit greatly from a visual component demonstrating the principles of good courtroom practices.

Computer

Computer technology is growing so quickly that it's starting to rival video in popularity. Computers can be used in distance education to deliver instruction, communicate asynchronously, research, and study.

Perhaps the most important thing to understand about computer delivery right now is how the computer can act as an integrator of disparate distance technologies. Surprisingly enough, because the computer can now bring together many technologies in one unified stream, it may be the technological medium that ends up most closely simulating the classroom environment for students at a distance.

For example, the World Wide Web already allows live text-based conferencing, live transmission of video and audio, and transmission of volumes of printed information. Right now, you can use the Internet to videoconference with someone hundreds of miles away, and the

F. Y. I.

VIRTUAL REALITY AT A DISTANCE

Chris Dede, professor of education and information technology at George Mason University, is widely regarded among distance educators as one of the best thinkers and futurists in the field. He has an uncanny ability to predict how emerging technologies will be used in education in the future. Years before anyone knew or dreamed about the World Wide Web, for instance, Dede predicted the widespread use of hypertext. He even managed to hint—correctly—at how it could be used.

One of his newest visions for the future involves employing virtual reality worlds as educational tools. Dede, along with several colleagues, has designed ScienceSpace, a group of virtual worlds that help students learn science principles. (Virtual reality worlds are realistic graphic simulations users can experience by wearing a headset.) There's NewtonWorld, MaxwellWorld, and PaulingWorld. In PaulingWorld, students can explore molecular structures from a unique bird's-eye view affordable via the virtual reality medium. Imagine investigating molecules as if you were an atom-size being, being able to poke, prod, and manipulate them. That's the idea of using virtual reality to learn.

According to Dede, what's great about virtual reality's use in education is not the great graphics or snazzy headsets students get to wear, but how virtual reality helps students learn by doing, thus enabling them to learn more, remember more, and ultimately use more of what they learn in real-life situations. And virtual reality environments don't have to be Hollywood-perfect to be super-effective. Watch for virtual reality environments to trickle into use within the next five to seven years.

technology that allows you to do this only costs about $100 (after the initial investment into a computer, modem, and peripherals).

There are three main streams of computer technologies: on-line computing, multimedia and software, and high-level integrated technologies such as virtual reality. Currently, distance programs most often use on-line options and software. In fact, on-line options are expanding extremely rapidly. Courses offered entirely over the World Wide Web and on-line schools are becoming as common as the Internet and the World Wide Web itself. And even more common is the pervasive use of e-mail for communication among distance learners and teachers as well as the use of the Web and BBSs for posting course information.

The computer has certainly added an extra dimension to distance ed. Let's take a look at your current options.

On-Line Options

Entire virtual colleges operate solely on-line, offering all courses electronically, via modem. You can get a master's degree, take a course, and meet people from all over the world simply by using your desktop computer and a modem. Even distance programs that rely on video, print, and audio technologies also use the on-line medium to enhance instruction. E-mail is the most popular supportive medium, with live computer conferencing also ranking high in importance.

The *World Wide Web* is a vast network of computers that anyone with a computer and a modem can access. The World Wide Web is a part of the Internet that allows for a more graphic delivery of information. Because the World Wide Web allows users to see text, graphics, and video and to hear audio all in one place, it has understandably become extremely popular for using in conjunction with distance ed.

Distance education varies in the way it uses the World Wide Web and the Internet. Some colleges and universities post schedules and class information on the Web, using it basically as a giant digital bulletin board for distance students. Some professors like to post extensive print materials on the Web. Other professors teach entire courses or parts of courses using the World Wide Web and the Internet. Languages and English composition courses are popular for this use, as are art courses. Other virtual colleges use special portions of the Internet to hold live "office hours" for distance students.

The World Wide Web hasn't been around very long, but already distance educators are experimenting wildly, trying to find ways of using the Web and the Internet to enhance students' distance experiences.

Private networks involve proprietary databases and systems that are available only to students. Private networks, not the Web or the Internet, are where almost all of the on-line teaching and learning leading to degrees and certificates occurs. The University of Phoenix On-line is an example of a private network. It contains databases, library access, messaging areas, and mailboxes. Students access the proprietary network using a computer and a modem. Typically, you need a password for access to the system, so that the on-line world at large is kept out.

Each private network uses a different operating system. This impacts how the screens look and operate. For instance, Windows 95, DOS, and Macintosh are operating systems for personal computers. Some operating systems for private networks are very simple, allowing only text communication. Other systems, like Lotus Notes, allows distance learners to watch video clips, see graphics, and also message each other and communicate on team projects—all while in the on-line environment. In general, private networks are not accessible via the Internet or the World Wide Web.

Private networks are useful for teaching courses with heavy reliance on words and still graphics to convey information. Management, business, language, math, science, engineering, and computer science are all excellent topics for on-line learning. They are very complete and contain significant databases of information, making them highly suitable for delivering intensive amounts of information. They're good options for teaching courses. Students report that person-to-person telephone calls become important when learning via this medium; it makes a real difference in establishing contact.

BBS (Bulletin Board System) allows users to employ a modem to dial into an electronic address where students can exchange messages and download information. In distance ed, colleges set up private BBSs to facilitate student communication at a distance. BBSs are rarely used as ways of teaching entire classes. Rather, they complement audio, print, and video delivery. The BBS facilitates inexpensive team communication and peer messaging.

For example, at the University of Alaska, students who have a computer and a modem can ask the instructor of a distance class to set up a BBS just for the class. Students can then access the BBS to exchange messages and work in teams. Only the class members have access to the BBS. A BBS used in this way is a simple type of private network.

E-mail, or *electronic mail,* is a way of using a computer and a modem to transmit text messages. On some computer systems, you can also transmit voice messages with the text. The real benefit of e-mail is that it isn't bound by geography in the same way that traditional mail is. You can send an e-mail message overseas and have it arrive in a matter of minutes. For geographically remote students, e-mail is a very reliable alternative to postal mail. And for all students, e-mail is a superb tool for asynchronous, or non-real-time, communication. Students report that they communicate well with teachers and peers via e-mail and develop good relationships without ever needing to pick up the telephone for a voice conversation.

I haven't yet found a class taught by e-mail, but I wouldn't be surprised if one were available. It seems, though, that the most popular use of e-mail is as a communication tool to support print, video, audio, and on-line computer delivery.

Computer conferencing, also called *live chat*, or if you're using the Internet, *Internet Relay Chat*, allows distance students to go on-line and type in real-time to each other. Like e-mail, this medium is best used as a supplement to instruction, not as a main means of instruction. Live on-line chat has one of the same advantages of live audio or videoconferencing, and that is immediacy. Of course, the drawback is that there are no visual or audio cues, so the communication, while immediate, isn't as information packed. On-line chat is extremely useful for accomplishing study and learning goals, however.

Another form is *desktop computer conferencing using computer networks*. One program in North Carolina uses desktop computer conferencing as a part of its courses. This option appears to be in the discussion phases at other universities; distance educators know about it, but they haven't moved on the technology yet. Don't be surprised to see this change dramatically in the future.

Multimedia and Interactive Options

Multimedia is just a snazzy way of saying that audio, text, and graphics are combined into one seamless package. Because only a relatively small percentage of people have CD-ROM players or other high-end computers that can handle multimedia packages, multimedia has been slow to catch on in distance ed. The main categories of multimedia include prepackaged and live. Let's look quickly at both.

CD-ROM technology allows massive quantities of information to be stored on CDs. CD-ROM is a prepackaged, nonlive technology. It is costly for distance institutions to develop CD-ROM courses, so few rely on this medium exclusively. The best use of CD-ROMs in distance ed is supplementary, or as hypermedia books.

Hypermedia include interactive books and documents. Hypermedia, though interactive, are not live. Essentially, the reader creates his or her own pathway through the material by choosing what he or she wants to

---

CU-SeeMe Around the World

Some distance programs have already experimented with CU-SeeMe technology. In 1994, the Open University in the United Kingdom set up a virtual summer school for an undergraduate course in cognitive psychology using CU-SeeMe technology as part of the course delivery method. Students attended the school electronically from their homes using a computer and modem.

The CU-SeeMe technology enabled students to watch multiple class participants from all over the globe, including a live virtual guest lecture by Donald A. Norman, a well-known cognitive science researcher. Combined with e-mail and computer conferencing, CU-SeeMe made for a highly interactive distance environment at a very low cost.

---

read (see the discussion of hypertext in chapter 7). No two readers will choose the same pathway. For example, a hypermedia book on the history of Western civilization may contain all the same chapters as a regular textbook, with certain key words and concepts developed in more depth. The reader, depending on his or her particular knowledge base, may or may not choose to explore all of the additional text.

CU-SeeMe

CU-SeeMe is a much-talked about, free, Internet-based videoconferencing program. Anyone with a Mac or a PC with Windows, a modem, and a Web-type connection can videoconference with other people who also have CU-SeeMe and a Web connection. CU-SeeMe uses the Internet to transmit live video images. What's exciting about CU-SeeMe is that you only need "beer" equipment to get "champagne" results.

Many distance educators are interested in CU-SeeMe technology. Elizabeth Jenkins, a senior research policy analyst for the New Mexico Commission on Higher Education, says that distance education has become a high priority for the state of New Mexico. According to Jenkins, she and other New Mexico legislators are watching Internet-based desktop video using PCs very closely.

Jenkins says that a sparsely populated, rural state like New Mexico needs to employ many distance options to reach all of the small, far-flung communities. CU-SeeMe might be just the low-cost interactive technology that will allow distance educators in New Mexico to bridge more distance gaps.

F. Y. I.

VIRTUAL REALITY ENVIRONMENTS

MUSE: Multi-User Simulation Environment
MUD: Multi-User Dimension
MOO: Multi-User Object-Oriented Environment

MOOs, MUDs, and MUSEs are interactive, text-based virtual reality environments. The main difference between them is simply what language rules the users employ while using them. As a note, MOOs, MUSEs, and MUDs differ from chat rooms in that MOOs, etc., are highly structured environments with specific rules for interacting. The conversation is very directed and purposeful. In a chat room, users simply make conversation.

While CU-SeeMe is a great technology, it is an immature one (it has only been around since 1992). Computer users can only use CU-SeeMe interactively point-to-point. Point-to-point means that one computer may videoconference and audioconference with one other computer. You can't, as of yet, videoconference interactively to multiple sites unless you have additional (and expensive) technology. But CU-SeeMe technology is very young, and you can bet that distance educators will continue to experiment with ways to take advantage of this window to the world.

MUSEs, MOOs, and MUDs

MUSEs, MOOs, and MUDs are text-based virtual reality environments originally created for playing word-based adventure games like "Zork" and "Advent." The great thing about these text-based environments is that multiple users can interact at the same place and time despite any physical distances.

It didn't take long for educators, distance and otherwise, to see the implications of the MOO, MUD, and MUSE technology. They began creating interactive learning environments immediately. While MOOs, MUDs, and MUSEs are not used extensively for distance education as of yet, there's lots of experimentation occurring. Look for these technologies to become more popular in distance classes.

Top Q's and A's About Virtual College

Here is a roundup of the most common questions people ask before they enter a distance program. You'll find the longer answers to some of these questions in other chapters. But here's the quick take on each.

- *Is it going to be too impersonal?*

   Your experiences as a distance learner will be studded with all sorts of personal interactions. Learning—at a distance just as in a classroom—is all about discussing, questioning, getting feedback, comparing notes, and clarifying ideas.

   You'll definitely interact with a teacher-facilitator. You'll also interact with classmates. With so many people in the picture, it's pretty difficult for a virtual education to be impersonal.

   More often than not, you'll discover that you get to know teachers and classmates better through distance education than in face-to-face education. The distance requires everyone to communicate extensively and effectively in order to succeed; you actually end up communicating more in a distance program than in most on-campus programs. (See chapter 4 for more details on this topic.)

- *I've been out of school for a while. Can I learn at the same pace I used to?*

   It is highly likely that your time away from school has made you a better, more able student. Even though you may feel rusty, distance education researchers have discovered that nontraditional students fare extremely well in their distance courses. Your work experience, life experience, emotional maturity, and independence will serve you very well, enhancing your ability to achieve academic success.

   Distance teachers say that your first days back in the classroom are the most critical for building self-esteem and academic confidence. The teachers I talked with said that communicating with them early on will help get you over your fears and into the class. Check out chapter 7 to see just how well distance students measure up.

- *Can I succeed if I'm not a super technical type?*

    Who is? In today's world, as soon as you master one brand-new technology, there's a newer gizmo being touted as the latest thing. Even those who think of themselves as technical types secretly admit that they aren't wizards in every area.

    If you're nontechnical, don't worry about it. You should obtain some level of technical proficiency, but don't let a fear of technology stand in the way of your education. Some distance classes simply require proficiency with the telephone and the U.S. mail. Others that require a little more expertise are still within your reach. Most important, many programs offer training; take advantage of it!

- *How much does my home equipment affect my choice of courses?*

    Your home equipment will only impact your choice if you take your classes from home. Some institutions maintain a fully equipped remote site with all the snazzy equipment you need. You may not need to purchase anything beyond a notebook and textbooks.

    If you will be taking courses from home, though, there's no getting around it: you will need to have the appropriate equipment. Ask the institution exactly what is required. If you don't have a particular piece of equipment and can't afford to go out and buy it, ask the institution if you can borrow what you need until you can purchase your own.

- *Will I ever interact with a real person, or will I be sending my material into a void?*

    Distance education is not the black hole of the education universe. You do not fax, e-mail, mail, phone, or otherwise send material "out there" only to have it sucked into a deep unknown. You will always have a human contact in your virtual education. Even when taking courses in which you are being graded by computer (which is rare), you'll still interact with a human being at many points in the course.

- *When can I access course information and take classes?*

    Some virtual colleges allow students to access courses and class information on demand. Others operate at a distance but on a regular schedule, like that of a traditional campus. You can expect to find the entire range of options.

If accessing a class at flexible hours is important to you, make sure that's the kind of course or program you sign up for. In general, video, on-line, and correspondence programs have the most flexible schedules; the least flexible programs involve interactive courses delivered live.

- *How can I learn a new course delivery method and course content at the same time?*

  Trying to overcome two obstacles at once is a lot like running full tilt up a mountain path. I've seen a few people do it, but those who do are in super shape and are usually professional athletes training for a specific sports event. Most everyone else hiking up a mountain adopts a moderate walking pace.

  Unless you are thrive on major challenges, master the course delivery (technology) first, then tackle course content. You will most often need to consider course delivery in on-line classes or in any class using a technology you're unfamiliar with.

- *I'm a people person. Will I get the personal feedback I need?*

  If you're a people person, make sure you're taking distance classes via a people-oriented medium that allows for lots of talking, working in teams, and frequent instructor contact. Your best bets will be live, interactive mediums such as videoconferencing and audioconferencing. Another good possibility is on-line classes with telephone conferencing backup. (See chapter 8 for more details on these technologies.)

- *Will distance education cost more and take longer?*

  Distance education doesn't have to cost more or take longer than traditional education. On the cost front, see chapter 5. Time-wise, your education will take as much or as little time as you want it to. Just as in traditional education, you can hasten or delay your graduation or completion date by taking more or fewer classes per semester or quarter. It's up to you.

- *What can I do to get the most possible transfer credits?*

  Whether or not you're at a distance, transferring credits is no easy task. The best advice is to push very hard for as many credits as possible. Let the institution know how serious you are about earning as much transfer credit as you can. (But remember: while you're pushing for credits, don't get pushy with the overworked admissions personnel!)

Find out who is responsible for evaluating your credits. Become more than a faceless transcript. Make contact, be courteous, and stay in touch as this person works with your records. When you're informed of what credits transferred in, you'll be in a position to request further action, if need be.

If only a few of your credits transfer, politely but firmly ask for further reviews. Don't feel you have to accept the first answer you get. After I earned my bachelor's degree, I applied to a different university as an undergraduate student. (I wanted to take some additional undergraduate courses before I went for my master's.) I was utterly stunned when I discovered that only 32 of my 215 credits transferred in!

Even though I wasn't trying to earn another undergraduate degree, just on principle I went to the vice president of the university and complained about the unreasonable lack of transfer credits. He ordered an immediate review of my transcript. After the review, the university accepted an additional 140 credits. While my situation was unusual, it points out just how bruising the transfer process can be. It also shows that you should always try to find avenues of further help if you aren't happy about your transfer process.

Keep in mind that some schools do have generous transfer agreements with community colleges and other state universities, virtually assuring you a 100 percent transfer rate. If you have lots of previous work you want to transfer in, it's in your best interest to find the "transfer-friendliest" school you can.

- *Is there such a thing as "life experience" credits for virtual college?*

Many virtual colleges grant credit for life experience—for military training, work experience, specific life experiences, and more. You won't be able to earn a complete degree with life experience credits, though. Typically, institutions set a credit ceiling of about 45 to 60 semester units. Still, that's a lot of credits to earn in one swipe.

It takes special skill to convince institutions to give you life experience credit. Don't go in without doing your homework first, or you'll be rebuffed. For more information about getting life experience credits, read *College Credit Without Classes: How to Obtain Academic Credit for What You Already Know,* by James L. Carroll (J. G. Ferguson Publishing, Chicago, IL, 1996). This is the most complete book on the subject I've found. It includes lots of practical information, with many examples and insiders' tips.

- *As a distance ed student, can I use my school's career counseling center?*

  Yes. If your institution has a resident career counselor or a career placement service, by all means take advantage of it. I know how easy it is to skip this step when you're getting ready to finish up your education, but if you find a good career counselor, that one phone call can significantly improve your chances of finding the job you want.

  Good career counselors are like walking libraries of résumé, interview, and job-hunting information. They're paid to be up on the latest résumé trends and tricky interview questions. And career placement services are pipelines to good opportunities in your field of study, particularly when you're attending a vocational school. In fact, many vocational schools pride themselves on their ability to place their graduates in jobs.

- *How do I list my virtually earned credit on my résumé?*

  You do not need to differentiate your degree, certificate, continuing education courses, etc., from the rest of your education by writing "earned off-campus" or another such phrase. Unless you want to play up the way in which you earned your certificate or degree, just list your distance-earned degrees or credentials as you do all other education. Otherwise, you may find yourself spending more time answering questions about your education than about your skills in interviews.

  However, if you work in a technology-related profession and you feel the skills you developed as a distance learner contribute to your ability to do the job, consider playing up those skills—especially if you earned your education on-line or via other advanced technology. On your résumé, list the distance education you earned with your other educational history. But in cover letters, discuss the special skills you gained from your distance learning and how they will be an asset to prospective employers.

- *How should I handle questions about my virtual education in interview situations?*

It's unlikely that you'll need to explain your distance education credentials unless you want to. But if an interviewer (or peer or employer for that matter) asks you about your education, don't get defensive. Remember: distance education is not second best. Maintain a confident attitude. You should be proud of your education. You have worked hard for it, and you know how much you've gained from it.

If interviewers or prospective employers don't understand the mechanics of your distance education, educate them. Bring them up-to-date and show them why they should snap you up in a hurry. Show them you bring special skills and qualities to the job as a result of your distance education.

Here are some suggestions for responding to questions and comments about your distance-earned education in interview or other work-related situations. Use these responses to turn a potentially negative situation around.

If an interviewer remarks, "I see you've earned your degree through independent study" or "Why didn't you get a regular degree?" you can respond with any one of these:

—*Distance learning is an extremely viable method of education. Distance learning is recognized by the American Council on Education and many other higher education organizations as completely legitimate.* (You can also mention that you attended a fully accredited program, if this is the case.)

Since I didn't have a teacher in the same room with me for motivation, I had to be particularly self-disciplined and self-motivated. As you can see by the fact that I completed my courses, I bring these and other positive qualities to the job.

—*As a distance learner, I worked with the latest technology. I earned my education, and I also became well versed in technology that brings my skills into the twenty-first century.*

Since distance education requires more participation than an on-campus education, I gained a great deal of experience articulating complex ideas efficiently.

—*Distance education is an effective way of continuing my education while still*

132

working. If you hire me, you know that I have the means, the skills, and the drive to stay competitive and up-to-date.

If your interviewer still doesn't budge, then go someplace where your distance education will be appreciated!

ON-LINE RESOURCES

You can access the on-line resources listed below via the World Wide Web. If you don't have access to the Web, you can look in your *Yellow Pages* under "Internet Services," "Telecommunications," "Computers—Networks," or "Computers—Multimedia" to find a company in your area that can provide you with a low-cost Internet or Web connection and tell you what specific equipment you need.

Your other option is to sign up with a major on-line service to gain Web access. This is the easiest way to hook up to the Web, but be warned that you'll pay more in the long run. Here are contact numbers:

- CompuServe: 800-848-8990

- America Online: 800-827-6364

Here are two excellent books on how to navigate the Web that won't leave you mired in technobabble:

- *Head for the Web*, Mary Jane Mara, Peachpit Press, 1996 (for Windows users).

- *WebHead*, Mary Jane Mara, Peachpit Press, 1995 (for Macintosh users).

Web Sites

Following are some excellent Web sites to visit. I have made every effort to provide accurate addresses; keep in mind, however, that they are subject to change. If you have difficulty accessing a site, check to make sure you are typing in the address correctly (remember, Web addresses are letter case sensitive). If you are unable to open a particular Web site, it is likely that the site has moved.

- **http://www.yahoo.com**
   Yahoo, as you may know, is a giant index of the Web. The Yahoo index is a super way to begin hunting for on-line information about distance education and available programs. At the Yahoo site,

you will find links to the newest virtual college programs, distance education associations, and distance education resources. As of this writing, Yahoo's distance education information is listed under:

- **www.yahoo.com/Education/On_Line_Teaching_ and_Learning/**

- You should also check under Yahoo's alternative education, adult and continuing education, and distance learning headings.

- **http://webster.commnet.edu/HP/pages/darling/ distance.html**

    This is another fabulous starting place for Web explorations of distance education. This page, created and maintained by professor Charles Darling of Capital Community-Technical College, is thorough and well organized. You'll find direct links to distance education discussion groups, distance learning associations, journals, and distance education providers.

- **http://www.uwex.edu/disted/home.html**

    This address is home to the University of Wisconsin's Distance Education Clearinghouse. Here you'll find links to information about University of Wisconsin programs as well as links to other information sources. The most compelling feature of this Web site is the long list of resources related to distance education.

- **http://www.intersource.com/~lifelong/dlsites.html**

    From the "Lifelong Learning Home Page" you can access listings of regionally accredited colleges and the distance degrees each offers. The list is by no means exhaustive, but it provides an excellent start. This site also contains links to the Distance Education and Training Council and other distance associations and organizations.

- **http://web.ce.utk.edu/**

    This is the University of Tennessee's Division of Continuing Studies and Distance Education site. You'll find information about

UTenn's program as well as many, many links to other distance education programs and resource lists.

- **http://www.nova.edu/Inter-Links/education/distance.html**
  Nova University's Web site offers numerous links to general distance education information as well as information about Nova's distance programs.

- **http://www.pbs.org**
  This is the PBS home page; here you can find a list of all community colleges participating in PBS's *Going the Distance* program.

- **http://www.wiche.edu**
  At the Western Cooperative for Educational Telecommunications Web site, you'll find many helpful documents relating to distance education; highlights include listings of new programs, the latest on the Western Virtual University, and many links to helpful documents and associations.

- **http://www.ed.gov**
  This is the U.S. Department of Education's Web site, an excellent place to find information about accreditation and federal financial aid.

- **http://www.petersons.com**
  Peterson's home page offers links to distance education resources, including books (such as this one) on distance education.

- **http://www.dc.enews.com/clusters/detc**
  This is the Web home of the Distance Education and Training Council. You will find links to member institutions as well as contact information on getting a free directory of accredited institutions.

- **http://www.caso.com**
  This site links to more than 2,000 Internet study resource sites as well as a near-comprehensive list of on-line college courses. You can also read profiles of accredited on-line course providers. Well worth a visit!

- **http://www.mit.edu:8001/people/cdmello/univ.html**
  This site is for the strong-hearted only. It lists, alphabetically

and geographically, the home pages of colleges and universities all over the world. No distinction is made between distance education and traditional education. Nevertheless, if you're trying to find general contact information for a college, you can try this site.

Discussion Sites

The main discussion site for distance education is the Usenet group **alt.education.distance**. In the on-line group, you can network with distance educators and other distance students by exchanging messages. To see a record of past discussions, you can visit the archives of **alt.education.distance** at:

gopher://burrow.cl.msu.edu/11/msu/dept/educ/edres/ newsgrp/alt.dised

You can open this address by typing in the address just like you would an http:// address.

Though other discussion lists do exist, many are scholarly and are not suitable for casual hobnobbing. Nevertheless, you may discover helpful information by reading. Here is one excellent electronic mailing list wherein top distance educators discuss the latest in the profession:

- **DEOS-L**
  This electronic mailing list is maintained by the American Center for the Study of Distance Education at Pennsylvania State University. Its purpose is to promote communication among distance educators and to disseminate information and requests about distance education around the world.

  To subscribe to DEOS-L, send e-mail to **LISTSERV@ PSUVM.PSU.EDU** with the message: **SUBSCRIBE DEOS-L your first name your last name**.

HIGH SCHOOL PROGRAMS

If you are interested in pursuing a high school diploma via distance education, here are two excellent programs, both widely accepted by colleges and universities. The diploma you receive from either of these programs will be treated as a "regular" high school diploma. Some private schools offer high school diplomas, but by and large they are not as widely accepted as diplomas from the two programs listed below.

Texas Tech University High School
Division of Continuing Education
P.O. Box 42191
Lubbock, TX 79409-2191
806-742-2352

University of Nebraska at Lincoln
Independent Study High School
269 Nebraska Center for Continuing Education
33rd and Holdredge Streets
Lincoln, NE 68583-9800
402-472-4321

DISTANCE EDUCATION RESEARCH

A good source for distance education research is *The American Journal of Distance Education*.

The American Journal of Distance Education
403 South Allen Street, Suite 206
Pennsylvania State University
University Park, PA 16801-5202

INDEX

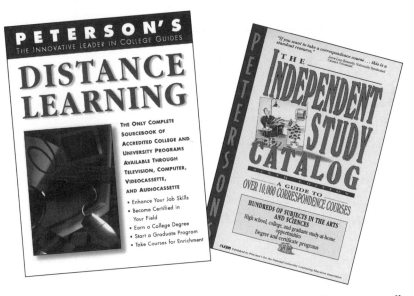